THE MILFORD SERIES
Popular Writers of Today

Volume Twenty-Two

A Poetry of Force and Darkness

The Fiction of

John Hawkes

by

Eliot Berry

R. REGINALD

THE Borgo Press

SAN BERNARDINO, CALIFORNIA

MCMLXXIX

For Eric Mottram and Geoffrey Wagner

81354
B45p
116410
Dec. 1980

Library of Congress Cataloging in Publication Data:

Berry, Eliot, 1949-
   A poetry of force and darkness.

      (The Milford Series: Popular Writers of Today ; v. 22 ISSN 0163-2469)
      Bibliography: p. 64.
      1. Hawkes, John, 1925- —Criticism and interpretation. I. Title.
PS3558.A82Z56   813'.5'4   79-282
ISBN 0-89370-132-7 (Library Binding; $8.95)
ISBN 0-89370-232-3 (Paperback Edition; $2.95)   OCLC #4591284

Produced, designed, and published by R. Reginald, The Borgo Press, P.O. Box 2845, San Bernardino, CA 92406, USA. Composition by Mary A. Burgess. Cover design by Judy Cloyd Graphic Design. Library binding by California Zip Bindery.

First Edition————May, 1979

PERSPECTIVE

The work of John Hawkes, like that of Nathaniel West, appears to be an anomaly in American fiction. Neither Hawkes nor West, a biography of whom Hawkes once started to write, can be limited by being called "an American writer." A "regional writer" from any country is limited, nationalism is just another form of provincialism, and a "national literature" is one that rarely deserves to be read outside the borders of its country. Hawkes, even more so than West, divorces himself from the recognizable American landscape—only *The Beetle Leg* is set in an American locale—the effort is to emphasize not the local or the personal but forces which have universal meaning.

Though not overtly political, Hawkes's work is, however, an effective barometer for a world which has become both intensely real and staggeringly imaginary, as the tension between what men have made and what men are as individuals has made the redefinition of the word "reality" an ongoing process.

If Hawkes can have any claim to being a "social writer", a writer concerned with the macrocosm and not just the individual, it is not in the sense that he tries to dramatize social problems in the manner of a Steinbeck, but in the more psychological sense by which Eliot suggested that the artist is metaphor for the society in which he lives: "The tension within the society may become also a tension within the mind of the more conscious individual." By the tenets of "popular realism", with its basic assumption that what is described in fiction is "real", Hawkes is an American heretic. From the beginning Hawkes was different from his American contemporaries, and it has only been in the last fifteen years that those recognized now as Hawkes's contemporaries—Barth, Barthelme, Coover, Gass, Pynchon and others—have entered, and in some instances surpassed, the territory that Hawkes was occupying a decade before.

The Cannibal (1949) if placed next to any other American novel about the war, and compared by language or structure, reveals Hawkes to be a radical from the very beginning. The vast majority of novels published in the United States since Hemingway belong to an enormous American fictional genre based on the popular notion that "simpler is better". This ill-defined idea, the merit of which has been tarnished by a million advertisements, is typified at the sentence level by a sparseness of prose that reached its zenith with Hemingway. The corollary to the "clean" truth that writers like Salinger and others tried to capture by the layering of simple declarative sentences, usually trimmed of adjectives and adverbs, was, apart from the simple-minded sentimentality of masses of books like Segal's *Love Story*, a far more significant underlying sense of constriction. In twentieth-century American literature there has been a reluctance to use the full orchestra, as if the very richness one could obtain between form, sound and meaning was corrupt or European. Hawkes, on the other hand, is much closer to James than Dreiser, and closest still to Faulkner. The richness of Hawkes's language is accompanied by a structural complexity that in turn has a metaphoric relationship to the writer's vision of the world in spatial, not linear terms. His prose, whatever its shortcomings or excesses may be, is an act of love most American writers seem afraid to commit with the English language.

It is in the area of language and a concern for form as metaphor for content that Hawkes stands apart from most American prose writers. The difference is not surprising given Hawkes's statement: "I would have been a romantic poet if I had not lived now" (Kuehl, *John Hawkes and the Craft of Conflict*, p. 171). Though the pervasive reality of the twentieth century may have turned poet to novelist, in many ways, structural as well as thematic, Hawkes is still a romantic. Hawkes's romanticism seems naturally to involve the imaginative artist's notion of love, with at times a gothic use of dream and subconscious forces. Hawkes says: "My fiction is almost totally visual, and the language depends almost totally on image. I think you're quite right that this fictional preoccupation and this particular interest in language do depend on my feelings for dreams and on my interest in exploiting the richness of the unconscious" (Scholes, *The New Fiction*, p. 103).

What exactly Hawkes means by "romantic poet" is not clear, but if one is to use his fiction as evidence, the formal standard would seem to be Eliot's *The Wasteland*. The elegant freedom of Hawkes's language is contrasted by the iron-grip of his form. The harmony Hawkes achieves out of this conflict is remarkable because, as in many American writers for whom conflict itself has become the end which historically is "resolution" for British writers, the conflict is deep within the writer himself: "On the one hand I am darkly committed to the puritan ethic. On the other I detest it and want to destroy it" (Kuehl, p. 164). This conflict requires Hawkes to exhibit a tightrope walker's skill in his fiction: he is able to resist subjectivity's special American form, the confessional novel, while at the same time plumbing the depths of the subconscious self.

Hawkes's understanding of reality as a strange mixture of the actual and the imaginary, the surface and the subconscious, requires a poet's distance and discipline which is best served by a language sufficiently flexible to give off meaning at more than one level. His care with language, his manipulation of novel form as if it were a poem, not only separates him from the prosaic writers of event and detail, but links him with a tradition that is as old in American literature as it appears to be radical in writers like Barth, Barthelme, Coover, Gardner and Vonnegut. Hawkes speaks to this tradition in *Insights:* "My novels are not highly plotted but certainly they're elaborately structured. I began to write fiction on the assumption that the true enemies of the novel were plot, character, setting, and theme, and having once abandoned these familiar ways of thinking about fiction, totality of vision or structure was really all that remained. And structure—verbal and psychological coherence—is still my largest concern as a writer. Related or corresponding event, recurring image and recurring action, these constitute the essential substance or meaningful density of my writing" (p. 156). Hawkes is not alone as an American novelist, for in various ways one finds a number of the most original and powerful American writers at this same junction of fiction and poetry—Brockden Brown, Hawthorne, Melville and West, to cite just a few. This tradition which now appears "new" in Barthelme's *Snow White* and *The Dead Father* or Gardner's *Grendel* is the tradition of that peculiarly American hybrid, the Romance Novel.

In many ways, Romance is where the Novel meets Poetry. When Hawkes talks of himself as a romantic poet, he hints at elements which connect his novels with the American Romance Novel tradition. As Richard Chase says in his *The American Novel and Its Traditions*: "American fiction has been notable for its poetic quality, which is not the poetry of verse nor yet the domestic or natur-

4

alistic poetry of the novel but the poetry of romance" (p. 17). Chase also finds that the element of romance in the American novel "since its earliest days" is a result of the "intense desire" of American writers from Brockden Brown onward "to drive everything through to the last turn of the screw or twist of the knife" a relentlessness which Chase suggests "distinguishes American writers from English and often results in romantic nihilism, a poetry of force and darkness," language which aptly describes Hawkes's work.

Chase's claim that "the history of the American novel is not only the history of the rise of realism but also the repeated rediscovery of the uses of romance" suggests a critical tie between Hawkes and the Romance novel, namely a redefinition of "reality" through the use of romance techniques and themes. The Romance Novel exists, as Hawthorne suggested in his Introduction to *The Scarlet Letter*, in "a neutral territory somewhere between the real world and fairyland, where the Actual and Imaginary meet, and each imbues itself with the nature of the other". If the experience of the 1960s and 1970s has taught us anything, it is that the "real world and fairy-land, the Actual and Imaginary" have met in the twentieth century and are forever joined. Chase offers a description of the word "romance" that applies most aptly to Hawkes's novelistic process: "let me say that the word must signify, besides the more obvious qualities of the picturesque and the heroic, an assumed freedom from the ordinary novelistic requirements of verisimilitude, development, and continuity, a tendency towards melodrama and idyll; a more or less formal abstractness and, on the other hand, a tendency to plunge into the underside of consciousness; a willingness to abandon moral questions or to ignore the spectacle of man in society, or to consider these things only indirectly or abstractly" (p. ix).

The appeal of romance is dualistic—to economy (as in a poem), yet also to greater depth. "Economy" and "depth"—the very words suggest the difference between romance and general fiction. Standard novels build horizontally and linearly, while the romance tends to portray the world in more vertical or spatial terms. The intensity is greater in the romance form. The qualities of "rapidity, irony, abstraction, profundity" that Chase cites are part of what makes the romance "an inevitable vehicle for the intellectual and moral ideas" of writers like Hawkes who refuse to depict simply "the spectacle of man in society."

Probably the most consistent way in which Hawkes aligns himself with the "romance novel" is his utilization of character and weaving of images. The relationship between author and character in romance is very similar to that between poet and image. Hawkes consistently succeeds in making images or metaphors out of his characters, and this abstraction, as Chase points out, is one of the keys to the symbolism central to the hybrid novel form as well as to romance: "The romance can flourish without providing much intricacy of relation. The characters, probably rather two-dimensional types, will not be completely related to each other or to society or to the past. Human beings will on the whole be shown in ideal relation—that is, they will share emotions only after they have become abstract or symbolic." This description of romance characterization sounds a great deal like Hawkes's own description of his goals in *The Blood Oranges*: "I wanted to create characters in total purity and to deny myself the novelistic easiness of past lives to draw on. It's easier to sustain fiction with flashbacks, with a kind of explanatory reconstruction of past lives . . . I wanted none of it."

It is in the handling of the two basic elements, character, and metaphor,

5

which in romance unlike the novel often seem to coincide, that the bond between Hawkes and his New England spiritual progenitor, Hawthorne, is strongest. Hawkes and Hawthorne share the romancer's dependence on symbol and metaphor to tell the story and to move it, a significant departure from the action built through scenes and character interaction. In this regard, Cyril's "weaving of the tapestry of love" is an important metaphor not only for *The Blood Oranges* but for all of Hawkes's work, for the weaving of language is essential to the process by which romancer conjures image and symbol into metaphor, a careful layering of language and idea akin to the leitmotif in music.

The effect of this layering and weaving is the creation of a sense of place out of what are basically objects. Just as in *The Scarlet Letter* the prison, forest, fireside, and scaffold are raised to metaphor, and convey a special sense of place, in *The Blood Oranges* Cyril's grape arbour, his wife's lemon grove, the twin villas separated by the funereal cypresses, the bus, the white ship, and the chastity belt all function as landmarks of the imagination. The metaphoric weight which both authors place on their words, coupled with the seemingly unconscious flow of prose which tends to equalize the effect of image and character, succeeds in making place function as character. Place, more than any individual in *The Cannibal*, provides a sense of humanity that gives the local its universal strength: "The town, roosting on charred earth, no longer ancient, the legs and head lopped from its only horse statue, gorged itself on straggling beggars and remained gaunt beneath an evil cloaked moon. Rattling trains turned back at the sight of the curling rails blossoming in the raw spring on the edge of town opposite the hill, and fields, plummeted with cannon balls, grew stained with the solitary needs of beasts and men" (*The C.*, p. 7).

The connection between Hawkes and Hawthorne goes past process and form to the very selection and coupling of words. In America, Hawthorne is the pioneering father of the language of paradox; Hawkes is a perfecting modern son. Paradox is the cornerstone of Hawkes's work. Indeed, he calls language: "the best way to make intangibility concrete. It's what's most characteristic of the human being . . . It's the highest form of paradox—and I like paradox."

James suggests that character "development" is essential to a novelist's process. If so, Hawkes is clearly not that kind of novelist. If the novelist, as James suggested, "is in the perpetual predicament that the continuity of things is the whole matter", the romance novelist, though perhaps longing for such a continuity, comes closer to the essential metaphoric relationship between form and content by creating characters in a fictional world closer to the actual twentieth-century experience, a reality which tends to isolate the individual into a grotesque parody of himself, and spin situation past him. Character still remains important for the modern romance novelist, for, manipulated as a metaphor, or floating in the neutral ground where incoherence meets understanding, character has become for the writer not so much a noun that marches out its destiny but a powerful adjective which illuminates more than itself. Characters like Hawkes's Census-Taker or Madame Snow in *The Cannibal* may seem Kafkaesque; Sparrow, Thick, Little Dora and Larry in *The Lime Twig* remind us of Dickens; but they all are prefigured by romance characters. A belief in character "development" is a belief in the possibilities of change, and most of the novelists of the 1960s seem wary of the prospects. While the situations around Hawkes's characters may change, the figures themselves change very little, being prisoners of their selves or the madness that surrounds them.

6

The modern romance novel approaches a New Realism, because, as Chase puts it, "In a romance much may be made of unrelatedness, of alienation and discontinuity, for the romancer operates in a universe that is less coherent than that of a novelist." Hawkes's romance realism is an effort to explore or otherwise understand the extremes that provoked James's perception that the element the early romances had in common was "the facing of danger," the voyeuristic American fascination with the way an individual responds to extremes has involved the American romance novel in two areas which greatly concern Hawkes: Love and the individual self. For Hawkes as for many modern writers, the situation now demands survival from two types of death, one the end of life, the other the end of sanity. The intersection of these two deaths is suicide. Hawkes does not sentimentalize suicide by making it an existential act—he sees no heroism in death of any sort—but this alternative is one which challenges almost all his primary figures.

In dealing with the "extreme situation" of sexuality, Hawkes has a great deal in common with Hawthorne. Hawthorne's relationship to Hester and her "A" is complicated. He turns her adultery into art and is obviously opposed to the society that forces her to wear it; yet somehow he is also threatened by her. The power of puritanism seems to provoke paradox. In Hawkes's work one encounters both a repulsion and attraction to the violence that seems inherent in sexuality; but, while Hawkes understands Passion as a force in opposition to Home and Security, and while he is able to make his language ring with a certain eroticism, this eroticism, steeped as it is in voyeurism and pain, is essentially sado-masochistic. Though he has profoundly understood both victim and victimization, there is such a complete lack of tenderness that one must really question whether Hawkes has thoroughly explored this territory. His primary concern seems to be with the ideas and aftermath of Desire and Passion, the sense of emptiness and loss; his characters rarely encounter the positive sides of sexuality and love. In this regard, one could call Hawkes's language either romantically poetic or repressed. Chase's insight into Hawthorne seems useful in understanding Hawkes: "In effect he admits that it is not only the poverty of materials in America that has led him, as he says in his prefaces, to write romances rather than novels, but also his puritan scruples—the romance allegory allowing him to treat the physical passions obliquely" (p. 55).

In *Second Skin* one gets meaning from the maze of images and metaphors in direct proportion to the amount one digs beneath the surface to make the elusive connections between image and idea. In *The Blood Oranges* and more strikingly in *Death, Sleep and the Traveler*, the process seems reversed. Ideas which used to hide in metaphors of thickly-layered sentences are often directly revealed in the trilogy. Here Hawkes offers the reader guidelines, words like "psyche", "the self", and "consciousness", which help the uninitiated to grasp what appeared earlier only as motorcycles, red wagons, race horses, and limes. While much of Hawkes's language here remains opposed to the realism of recorded detail, authorial self-consciousness seems to have shifted the burden from the *suggestion* of image and metaphor, the romance way, to the more prosaic method of *telling* usually associated with the novel. In *Second Skin* one can recognize the possibilities of self-awareness and change within the individual—accompanied by an increase in the perceptions of the first person narrator—one senses as well the shift in Hawkes's work away from the romance back towards the novel proper.

The fiction before *The Blood Oranges* more closely resembles the rope-free balloon of the romancer that James refers to in his Introduction to *The American*: "The balloon of experience is in fact, of course, tied to the earth, and under the necessity we swing, thanks to a rope of remarkable length, in the more or less commodious car of the imagination; but it is by the rope that we know where we are, and from the moment that cable is cut we are at large and unrelated . . . The art of the romancer is, 'for the fun of it', insidiously to cut the cable, to cut it without our detecting him." Though Hawkes tends to bring the balloon of the imagination back down to earth in his trilogy, by the conscious addressing of the question of "sexuality and the romantic imagination", the cable is effectively cut for most of his early work. Behind the romance elements that distinguish Hawkes's work are forces which link this apparent "wild child of American fiction" to concerns that, despite the imaginary landscape, are essentially American. As Olderman points out in *Beyond the Wasteland*: "There are two essential differences between romance in the novels of the 1960s and traditional American romance . . . [First] the confused concept of reality motivated by a blurring of fact and fiction. The second is the controlling metaphor that attends the impulse to romance . . . if the contemporary American novel continues to employ the devices of romance, it must also continue to employ some controlling metaphor. In the past critics have pointed out that American literature is informed with the metaphors of a 'lost Eden', the 'American Adam', and 'the American Dream' . . . It is not true of the 1960s which finds its controlling metaphor in the image of the wasteland."

And yet, though in almost every novel Hawkes's imaginary landscape resembles a wasteland, one senses an analytic nostalgia for a lost innocence of near mythic proportions. This loss of innocence, most visible in his collection of plays, *The Innocent Party*, and most powerful in the impenetrable space that separates Margaret from Michael Banks in *The Lime Twig*, is not sentimental. On the contrary, the emotions are dissected with an almost scientific precision, and this combination of authorial distance with all that a loss of innocence can entail is a key to Hawkes's particular strength as a writer.

THE EARLY LANDSCAPES: REPRESSION AND EXPERIMENTATION
CHARIVARI (1949), *THE GOOSE ON THE GRAVE, THE OWL* (1954)

"Like the poem, the experimental fiction is an exclamation of psychic materials which come to the writer all readily distorted, prefigured in that nightly inner schism between the rational and the absurd." (Notes on The Wild Goose Chase)

There is a sharp contrast in Hawkes's three short novels between the repression that one encounters in the world, and the act of freedom suggested by the creative act of experimentation, the depiction of reality in essentially metaphorical rather than linear terms. This apparent paradox reflects both Hawkes's belief that paradox "lies at the center of the imagination; imagination probably could not function without some such paradox of opposites," and the paradox contained deep within the writer himself: "My background is New England puritanism. I suppose that I have been trying to write my way out of that terrible fictive burden of guilt, guilt is clearly what is wrong with everything" (*TREMA*, Paris III, p. 271).

Though Hawkes is not overtly trying to write himself out of this paradox—"the fiction isn't aimed at myself . . . I'm not concerned with my own life or interests. I'm simply trying to create a new world, a new landscape in order to use the language in some newly necessary way"—the movement between *Charivari* and Cyril's "song of sexual freedom" in *The Blood Oranges* reflects both at the level of the imagery and in the authorial point of view a change at the very source. While Hawkes prefers to see the landscapes he has created in terms of their more lasting meaning, the act of "experimental" rather than "confessional" fiction, the responsible writer is always the subconscious of his words.

In discussing the American writers with whom he feels a particular kinship—Nathaniel West, Djuna Barnes and Flannery O'Connor—Hawkes writes: "Like the poem, the experimental fiction is an exclamation of psychic materials which come to the writer all readily distorted, prefigured in that nightly inner schism between the rational and the absurd" (*Notes on the Wild Goose Chase*, p. 249). Hawkes's understanding of the experimental fiction as a poem which grows out of "the schism between the rational and the absurd," inevitably breaking down the arbitrary distinction between dream and reality, places his early fictions solidly within the parameters of the romance novel. Utilizing the dream-exaggeration of character usually associated with surrealism (but also a key to romance structures), these novellas are early evidence of Hawkes's challenge to standard fictional structures. By American fiction standards at the end of the '40s and early '50s, these innovative fictions represent a radical departure, particularly when placed in the context of the Eisenhower years and McCarthyism.

The first of these experimental works, *Charivari*, written for Albert Guerard's writing class at Harvard (as was *The Cannibal*, which Hawkes began the following term, 1948) remains a flawed, precocious, potential-laden manuscript. In its way, the novel, like many first novels, verges on self-examination in the guise of fiction. Hawkes has said that his background is New England puritanism, and this background is evident both in the sterility of *Charivari*, the distance that separates Henry and Emily, and in the bitterness of the portrayal of the guests at the wedding party, humour in rebellion.

Though there are neither characters nor scenes that develop in the sense that James and George Eliot presume that characters do and should develop; despite the surface strangeness of the manuscript, the movement of the novel is not fundamentally vertical, as with Hawkes's work from *The Cannibal* forward, but horizontal, as in standard non-romance fiction. Were it not for the relatively radical suggestion that Happiness means *not* having a child, the ending of *Charivari* reads like that of many standard novels which build Time and Situation to a crescendo, ending with what, in light of the essential uncertainty of twentieth-century reality, may seem a naive resolution: "When she ran across the lawn, hair loose flying, colored skirt whirling about her knees, he knew that she was not going to have a child. The flowers around her neck were wet with dew, and as she ran she laughed, and her face was momentarily bright.

'My goodness,' thought Henry, 'she does look young!' She ran quickly towards him.

Gaylor blew loudly on his whistle. 'All right,' he called, 'it's time to play' " (*LL* p. 136).

Charivari, which means a mock serenade of discordant noises usually made for a newly married couple to show disapproval of the wedding, is divided into four parts: "Courtship", "The Bachelors", "The Wedding," and "Rhythm". Though fragmented, a plot implying a movement from beginning to end is part of the discernible progression in *Charivari* from separation to union. Henry and Emily experience a series of events—a weekend houseparty, a bus journey to a seacoast town, the wedding and its aftermath—some more hallucinatory than others, that contribute to the breakdown in the reader's mind of the conventional distinction between dream and reality. The characters encountered are grotesque—the "ruddy monster from South America", the "determined unnamed adventuress in green", "an ungracious daughter", "vicious little Noel", and the harmless homosexual, Gaylor—their flatness speaking not only to their limitations as human beings, but also to the absurd air of comedy that pervades the whole situation. The two sets of parents—Henry's meek mother Beady and his puritanical parson/father, and Emily's seven foot tall father and nagging mother, the General and Mrs. Soris Smithson Valentine—represent a grotesque, puritanical past that anyone would want to escape. Henry buses to a seaside town to escape the encompassing morality, but can neither sleep with the woman in black (who reminds him, like guilt, of Emily), nor return to Emily without the morality enforced by his father's visit. Back home, Emily pays a collier's wife to make her a wedding gown, but what emerges from this scene, in which the seamstress stabs the bust of the wedding dress, is a sense of fear that is magnified when Emily has a medical examination and imagines herself a prisoner, the doctor's probing hallucinated as violation by a riveter's gun. The title is thus appropriately derisive of such a union: little has changed or been positively overcome.

Charivari is written in the third-person omniscient narration that one senses was essential for the establishment of distance between the young writer and Henry, the central figure; the story begins with a dream that is a forerunner to the blend of dream and reality that distinguishes all of Hawkes's work. The opening sentence is told in dialogue like a play between Henry and his subconscious "Expositor," whose primary function is to challenge Henry's existence—"What time is it Henry? . . . What should you be doing?" (*LL*, p. 51). It raises questions which move the narrative from the dutifully invoked anal vision—"Expositor: Come on; we'll take you to clean the stables.
Henry: Must I do it with my hands?"—to an image, Woman, which from the outset is associated by Hawkes with deception and jealousy—"Expositor: What is she doing? Henry: Making love to the stable boy while I do his work" (*LL* p. 52).

This early evidence of an innate distrust of women makes Woman an object of some loathing ("She . . . the impersonal, everlasting she" [*LL*, p. 53], and the animosity in this male-female relationship—"she felt a pleasing depression, the warm sensation of being ignored"; "they seemed irresistibly drawn into the negative contemplation of each other" (*LL* p. 88)—offers insight into much of the pain in Hawkes's subsequent portrayal of love. Love is at the centre of Hawkes's dualism, and Woman emerges as the original symbol of man's dilemma: Henry's need for love is commensurate with his need for security; Emily is a threat to Henry until it becomes clear at the end that she is not going to have a child, and Henry is assured, as with many of Hawkes's male figures (Camper, Hencher, Hugh) of having both wife and mother in the same woman. Childhood fears are used in *Charivari* both as a source of Imagery—" 'Hello, mother,' Henry whispered. A thousand hands reached up for him at once. He was a gaunt, cut-up, timid little boy."—and as a basis for the central fact that no matter what age Henry really is, he remains fundamentally a son.

The evidence of this need for wife/mother is seen in an incest taboo: while Henry wants Emily primarily as a security figure, a Mother, he is repulsed by the idea of being with her, a conflict which unites and separates them in much the way as Banks in *The Lime Twig*: "Drawn to her, he fled from her" (*LT* p. 88). Throughout Hawkes's work, the male often has unspoken sexual difficulties, especially with his wife, who also represents the mother/security figure. Indeed, the forty-year-old child worries about his masculinity: "Why must I always play the feminine role? Why don't they come and change my pants?" (*LL* p. 71). Other women are the objects of lust or momentary desire, but until *The Blood Oranges*, there is little evidence that even desire can be positive.

Elements of sexual repression and puritanism run through all of Hawkes's work. Hugh has his origins in *Charivari*'s Henry, a figure the older Hawkes is at pains to overcome. The physical attraction for something that is spiritually *verboten* is what gives the sexual aspect in Hawkes its special colouring, and this edge of repression, which is the basis for the almost voyeuristic air in his descriptions of pain and pleasure, is as much in evidence in the young Hawkes as it is in *Travesty*. The celery-eating scene in *Charivari*—"She opened her mouth. He stuck the oval between her lips, the spongy stalk protruding out with its droopy, yellow leaves" (*LL* p. 58)—is almost identical to the scene written twenty-five years later in *Travesty* in which the father enjoys watching his daughter nibbling at the dangling carrot: "Well, the admirable young contestants searched in vain, caught the tips of the carrots between eager lips, screamed joyously, thereby once again losing the prize. The carrots began to glisten . . . it was Chantal, of course, who finally understood the game and slowly, sinuously, drew the carrot between her lips and sucked, chewed, reaching always upward with her small lovely face, until the deed was quite beautifully done" (*T* pp. 118-19).

Liberated in its way, for its time, *Charivari* is testament that from the beginning Hawkes recognized the dangers inherent in marriage, clearly understanding the fear of enslavement a woman may have; Emily, prefiguring Margaret Banks, "wanted to scratch her nose beneath the veil, but each of her wrists was pinioned at her sides by firm, unrelaxing fingers. The blindfold pressed into her eyes . . . " (*LL* p. 123). Here again, where there appears to be sympathy, there is also evidence of an almost sadistic pleasure in woman's plight; in a dream that Henry has towards the end, Emily is portrayed like Margaret in a state of pain and imprisonment; Emily, however, gets no pleasure from the pain. Henry imagines a hospital matron levelling "a large atomizer into Emily's face. A harsh red liquid squirted into her eyes and immediately a cotton fuzz grew about her skull, covered the walls and floors and sealed her eyeballs in a filmy crust. One hand on her stomach, the other over her burning eyes, she ran on . . . " (*LL* p. 129).

Perhaps most relevant to Hawkes's later work is the fact that both Henry and Emily first appear in the semi-conscious state of sleep. Neither awake nor asleep, conscious or unconscious, each is in his separate room, "A massive dog patrolled the space between" (*LL* p. 51). This "space between", both in *Charivari* and in Hawkes's later work, is the novelist's primary area of concern, the grey area of human purgatory, an inextricable combination of heaven and hell. The patrol of the "massive dog", associated with the emptiness between people, is absolutely essential to Hawkes's work; for the dog image, multiplied here into a "pack", comes to symbolize in Hawkes the space *within* the individual where the mixture of dream and reality, conscious and unconscious, threatens security to the point of madness. This is the battlefield, and there are few surviving heroes. The implication in *The Blood Oranges* is that he who can positively control, manipulating rather than trying to repress the forces within, may avoid Hugh's fate. In *Charivari*, this control is a result less of the process of understanding than an imposed means by which the author overcomes the area that separated Henry and Emily. The imposition of the author's will does, however, offer a nice formal reprise to the invocation of the "massive dog" on the first page; by the end of *Charivari*, the dogs, like the puritanical madness that fills the emptiness between Henry and Emily, are seemingly under control: "The gardener with his striped trainman's cap and mudcaked overalls eyes the dogs, put the horn to his mouth and sent shrill strains across the morning countryside, calling the pack" (*LL*, p. 135).

In spite of the evidence in *Charivari* of Hawkes's paradoxical relationship to puritanism—the source of pain as well as creativity in his work—his repeated insistence on authorial detachment is not to be dismissed; this detachment succeeds in liberating the narrative voice, first person or third, and in so doing, leaves the reader free, unaided but uninfluenced, to float in that purgatory Hawkes creates between dream and reality. If one agrees with Theodore Reik that "Recollection is conservative; memory is destructive," Hawkes's early novels are neither destructive nor conservative. *The Goose on the Grave* evokes a modern war, but as in *The Cannibal*, creativity (the freedom of language and form)triumphs over the repressive world simply because the novel is not a picture or a memory of something past, but rather something that through the metaphors underlying the event is preserved in the calendar of history. The strength of Hawkes's creative decision is that, by concentrating his focus on the subterranean forces at work inside the microcosm of the world (the individual), his reader is confronted with the problems of history at their source. History is the waste product of people.

Though Hawkes has called his move towards Guerard's notion of Realism inevitable—and given the realities of writing in America, some such shift was probably necessary—these two early fictions offer a reminder of a direction Hawkes might have followed. In the use of character as metaphor and image as plot vehicle, in the raising of local to universal through the non-obtrusive growth of image and place into metaphor, in the way reality is made part of an ongoing dream, the lesson of *The Goose on the Grave* and *The Owl* is the key to the success of all his early novels.

One can see in these two novellas exactly the difference between Hawkes's early and late work. The imaginative acts could not be more different. Behind the early works—at least through *The Lime Twig*, at times in *Second Skin*—there is the sensation that there is something enormous beneath it all. This force—call it the war or the writer's subconscious—is a well. Initially the author seems to take care never to write directly about the source. Rather, event is filtered through image as in a poem, so that the resulting fiction is neither mired in a conventionally realistic depiction of the war, nor oozing with the problems of personal conflict. As in Hawthorne's romances, the personal is present in James's sense of "felt prose," yet character and image are so naturally woven into metaphor that the local is raised to the level of universal.

Set in Italy during the war, *The Goose on the Grave* gives the reader neither the insights of a first person or the "third-person-close" narrator; one is generally unaware of the two opposite armies and the two generals. Rather one is immediately confronted with a larger, more universal scope, with the signs of struggle and survival. Instead of stating the problem, Hawkes finds as objective correlatives images and edifices whose strength lies in the fact that they are capable, like the forest, the scaffold, and Hester's "A" in *The Scarlet Letter*, of a whole range of metaphorical possibilities.

In *Goose on the Grave* one encounters, for instance, not a battlefield, but a bakery and a hospital which "joined at the end of a narrow street blocked with carts upon which casualties lay in the sunlight" (*GG*, p. 201). The dryness of the marching soldiers, the aridity that war spreads over the land and through the people, is suggested by the description: "the baker's women in the morning brushed flour from their bosoms, out of their hair, and the white sack dresses sagged slackly over nakedness." The bakery, a symbol of plenty now turned to emptiness, grows to powerful proportions through skillful repetition—the drops of water that roll across Adeppi's blanket—and association. The emergence of the well raises the water/dust metaphor to the level of sexuality, particularly in terms of young Adeppi: "The women dipped the buckets one by one from the well . . . Adeppi sat on the rim of the well" (*GG* p. 210). In building the local into the universal through an unobtrusive metaphorical weave, it is the lack of detail, the apparent lack of specificity, that allows the words, like the sense of Time, to take on their larger value; in the following quote, the "state" could be any state, the "city" any city that is besieged by the forces which dry out life: "During the state's year of dissolution, the chains across the city gates were smashed and smoke rolled in from the sea and across the mountains. Hardly awake, the baker's women . . . " (*GG* p. 201).

Both novellas are set in the time of no-time that gives the reality of Romance its ongoing quality of dream. The sense of wounded Time is beautifully conveyed at the outset by the open wound of the pink stone—"The stone was pink, the salmon color of long inactivity" (*GG* p. 201). The sense of universal Time is supported by the shifts in narrative focus which never allow one individual to dominate the horizon, and by moments, interspersed, that remind one of the painful reverberations of Time: "Nino's wounds had healed; the guitar warped on its peg" (*GG* p. 207). One encounters also the dialogue which distinguishes Hawke's work through *The Lime Twig*, phrases which seem to hang in a dream: " 'Secrets. And I suspect,' Dolce's words came cold and accusing, after a moment, 'no saint to guard your nights.' "

In *The Goose on the Grave* one can see the origins of several of Hawkes's later images and themes, the use, for example, of animals, cows, horses, and dogs to convey the human condition. As suggested by the hospital and Jacopo's cry of "Infermo, infermo!" (*GG* p. 228), there is a sickness in the land and in the people which is both a byproduct and a source of the war. The sickness is sexual sterility and its resulting violence, war. The sickness is virtually impossible to avoid, as Jacopo, the accordion player, and Adeppi, the child who sings, discover. Jacopo is beaten by two carabinieri who threaten to induct him, and although he is released, the damage may be done, for the child has been forced to witness the violence of adults. As in *The Cannibal* and *The Beetle Leg*, dogs are used to convey this sense of madness stalking across the land: "The gray dogs, in pursuit but not marauding, ran through this summer afterdark; slowed to a sudden trot, they stalked across the empty trysting places, then off again, jowls fastidiously dripping ground meal and bone" (*GG* p. 254). The metaphor for hungered madness is skillfully handled, the force the dogs represent abating only at the sound of life and love—when the mandolin plays "The dogs were gone" (*GG* p.256).

The beauty of Hawkes's romance lies in the way images and characters are connected through metaphors which bind the interior of the novella with both image and idea. The dryness of the bakery, associated with the sickness of the hospital and opposed by the sexuality of the well, grows through the description of the cow belonging to the contessa's mother to the extent that cow and mother become one in terms of dried-up fertility that is spreading across the land: "The earth was her pedestal. Her horns were hollow. She had turned gray wading across the fields and now lay with back caved as if under blocks of stone, two delicate forelegs doubled beneath her breast in the straw . . . Her whole face was swelled about the tongue which grew large, as did her haunches, while she guarded the stucco and statuary of a milkless past" (*GG* p. 233). Even the contessa's mother is sterile: "The old woman removed her short jacket, her narrow skirts, until she stood in nothing but a sleeveless hair shirt, old and worn, a thin brown penitent garb that clung to her body . . . Long ago it had been stitched unevenly up the front and little punishment remained in it" (*GG* p.234). This connection between the contessa and dryness is the key to the political and sexual repression which although never mentioned overtly, is the power behind the novella.

In contrast to the contessa, Arsella is a force not unlike Hester, for she is born outside the law, and not let inside the church, which in Italy as in Puritan America can be seen as a symbol of secular as well as religious law: "Arsella was born in a vineyard, was found to be a girl by an old man nearby and was carried in her mother's arms—a throng met them in the village—to the steps of the church, not inside" (*GG* p. 237). As a force of the wilderness she is linked to Adeppi, who is Hawke's first polluted innocent; but the forces of repression and war, as suggested by the contessa, the cow, the bakery, and the hospital, triumph. Music is distorted: "The music stopped short. None such had been heard since the closing of the Gutto, no such frightening sound as that of music moving across the barricaded-off quarters of a silent city, across the back houses, gardens and chimneys" (*GG* p. 227). Sexuality is denied.

Jacopo and Adeppi have already met the carabinieri, violent symbols of the State. Hawkes goes on to suggest through the opposition of Adeppi (the singing of the boy who sets on the edge of the Water) and the priest (voice of morality) that the cause of this conflict is based on the morality of the other paternal institution, the Church.

The repression of religion is most devastatingly seen in man's relationship to woman. Just as the priest would have his "children" worship the image of Christ, Nino places Bianca Maria on a pedestal. Nino captures the image, but, as will be the case with Hugh's peasant nudes in *The Blood Oranges*, the photographic image is sterile—Bianca Maria runs into the bakery after posing. In Adeppi's dream, "Nino the fatherless" soldier cries out: "It will not heal! It will not heal, fratello mio" (*LL* p. 235). The connection between Image, Woman, Artist and Repression is particularly powerful given the evidence that the young soldier is actually driven mad by the frustration: " 'Stop the noise,' commanded Nino. The pistol was pressing against Adeppi's ear . . . Nino's wild figure stood quivering by the hooded well" (*GG* p. 211).

Repression, the confict within man based on one's inability to find an outlet commensurate to the love of woman's image, the interior wasteland behind the exterior wasteland of the war, is the reason that humanity has been reduced virtually to the level of insects ("Look how they crawl, Arsella!" [*GG*, p. 253]). With the reemergence of the power of the priest Adeppi is ultimately condemned by the crowd, "O sacrilegio, sacrilegio!" (*GG* p. 274) in much the same way as Hester is—madness is loosed again: "Gray dogs came out of their dens." As in Kafka, the pressure of repression has become so severe that the line between dream and reality is effectively snapped: "Under his hands, behind the face, deep inside the dark sac of the brain, he dreamed of them and it persisted, a continuous dream, warm and without waiting and despite the presence across the valley of the enemy" (*GG* p. 275).

The Goose on the Grave ends with "the enemy," introducing the fundamental question of just who "the enemy" is. The evidence in *The Owl* seems to suggest that "the enemy" is the authority figure, which in *The Goose* is the priest, and in *The Owl*, the hangman. In this regard the situation of *The Owl* is more complex because the authority figure is also the narrator, a striking example of the recurring relationship between author, repressive narrator, and narration that Hawkes defends by saying: "I find paradox everywhere. On the one hand my fiction depends on a kind of cold, detached, authoritarian stance which I could think of as puritanical, but in so far as the fiction is personal it is so only in the sense that I'm interested in destroying puritanism, overcoming puritan morality" (Kuehl, p. 158). In the case of *The Owl*, Hawkes's distance and control is exemplary. The narrator's control is such that, although he is called "Il Gufo," and thus is inextricably linked to the owl, the author is capable of separating himself from both the owl and the narrator. Hawkes says of this narrator: "The first-person narrator of *The Cannibal* was, in a sense, merely mechanical. *The Owl* was written in the first person to rewrite *The Cannibal*" (Keuhl, p. 163). Indeed, Il Gufo seems to emerge just where Zizendorf leaves off, as a God—or as Hawkes puts it, "the narrator of *The Owl* emerged as a godlike voice rather than the articulated personality of a genuinely created character." It is this absence of "articulated character" that is responsible in part for making *The Owl* a remarkable experiment in fiction, for the novella is a romance with a first person narator who is more image than man. The metaphor that the image of the owl becomes is Repression. The further one stretches the image, the more the metaphor grows. The owl swoops down on its helpless prey, and like Hawkes himself, the owl can see in what remains darkness even for the narrator. One is rewarded for examining *The Owl* as a Romance.

The central image of the owl/hangman reflects in its exaggeration the junction of the grotesque and Romance. Indeed, the power of the hangman for the citizens depends precisely on this exaggeration of the image, and Hawkes clearly suggests that the relationship between Image and Power—as any campaign poster is testament—represents exaggeration to grotesque proportions, if not actually to perversion: "The hangman shall be four cubits tall or more, shall have a head of prominent bones and smooth on top so that all admire the irrevocable round of the bone and largeness of brain . . . he shall wear a pointed black cap the better to see him and to make the grimness of his nature apparent by contrast with the conical black peak, in the manner in which the fiercest animals are fashioned with some unnatural largeness of hindquarters, stripes on their sides, or horn" (*The Owl*, p. 157). Not surprisingly, the hangman believes in the preservation of the Image; as authority figure, he cannot tolerate the disfiguration of the Image of Woman as Virgin—"I saw the defamation, the

Donna's face smeared with blood, I galloped. As I passed her, I raised my boot and, ramming her chest, dislodged her so that she fell and rolled upon the crackle of the clearing" (*O*, p. 163). Yet, as we shall see, his belief in the pure Virginity of Woman is part of his repressive nature. There are primarily three forces at work in this romance: the Hangman, the Citizens, and the Prisoner. The novella begins much as *The Scarlet Letter* does with a description of the prison, here called the *fortress*. The fortress, the hangman's property, emerges as a presence through repetition and the uncluttered place it holds on the fictive horizon: "The further I rode from the city of Sasso Fetore, the better was the view of the fortress, large and silhouetted, black and irregular up there . . ." (*O*, p. 162). The dream reality of *The Owl* is signalled by Il Gufo's reference to "the meal, torn from the anatomy of conscience" (*O*, p. 197); and the romance raises important questions about the nature of repression, for, if it is a dream, it is the citizens of Sasso Fetore that live out the dream.

As a shape in the dream and a symbol of repression, the fortress is equally dominated by Il Gufo and the "monarchical owl" (*O*, p. 194). The irony of the repressive nature of the hangman is the dependence of the citizens on this authority figure: "But the old men of Sasso Fetore needed to talk of their hangman" (*O* p. 140). So deep-rooted is the repression that it seems a natural force—"Rain . . . imprisoning Sasso Fetore behind the thickened jambs" (*O*, p. 141). As in *The Goose on the Grave*), the nature of this repression is primarily sexual—"that one wretched mass of the sex was about to rise to the temptation" (*O*, p. 152); girls must remain images of the Virgin. The hangman puts his assistant to work "kneading my virgin rope coils," and he appreciates the connection between death and the preservation of the Image. The denial of the sexual outlet is the source of authoritarian violence in *The Owl* just as it seemed to be the source of conflict behind the war in *The Goose on the Grave*: "The girls were not merely virgin, those unseen propagated a sense of timelessness of denial, of death hung rocking around and around on the broken-spoked wheel atop a pole. Little Ginevra was kept at home" (*O*, p. 140). The dogs reappear, but even these symbols of madness are repressed: "The dogs tasted of blood given in mean measure but were not permitted the latter, the howl, the reckless male letting of their species. Beaten across the quarters, they were taught by the monks the blind, perfectly executed gavotte" (*O*, p. 182).

The triumph of *The Owl* is the connection Hawkes makes between the hangman and his prisoner. The connection, when one places two sections of *The Owl*'s narration side by side, is not simply the natural paradox of polar forces—the inevitable link between victim and victimizer—but seems to have its origin in the romantic vision of the author. The two passages, among the most lyrical in all of Hawkes's fiction, seem out of place spoken by this demonic authority figure, until one recalls that the image of an unattainable woman is the source of the romantic's pain. The image of woman which denies natural outlet is what makes the Hawkesian romantic a prisoner. The first passage is the tenderest in Hawkes's fiction: "At last we reached the ledge and stood side by side, then face to face so that I could not mistake her, Antonina. Not from weariness she leaned against the lower walling of the fortress morticed agedly into the cliff. Already her breast was rising and the noon fled. We had no need to whisper, not even the birds were within rock's throw. But the wind was in our faces and we were temporary, though Antonina did not look as if her heart were sinking. The world this high creaked around us and, standing with no sure footing between the day before and the day after, she touched her bosom done with lightheartedness, spoke to me in the wind's way . . . What was there more?" (*O*, p. 184). "There was the prisoner", Hawkes replies, and his subsequent lyrical description of the prisoner as a bird makes the connection, primarily through the tone of the passage, between two parts of this romantic vision, the image of beauty and the prisoner of the Image in flight: "He brought his knees into the pit of his stomach and climbed toward open sky. The prisoner hovered, turned awkwardly, swooped over our heads—he kicked the air as he dove!—and sailed in a long arc up again, around, about to disappear . . . I saw him lastly fly defiantly through the smoke of Monco's deserted fire and into the red sun that sank and drew him down over the edge of the earth" (*O*, p. 186).

If one does not attribute the lyricism of such a passage to an inconsistency in the narration, if one accepts that Il Gufo is capable of imaginative/descriptive flight—the description of Antonina reflecting passion, that of the prisoner's flight reflecting an appreciation akin to sympathy—the bond between prisoner and hangman becomes tight. Prisoner and hangman are one in the rhythm of desire and repression. The hangman's desire for Antonina is the freedom that was the prisoner's crime. The hangman, however, insists on the difference, the legal morality: Antonina wants to marry the hangman, whereas there is no indication that the prisoner would ever contemplate such a legal/moral sanction.

The Blood Oranges and *Death, Sleep and the Travler* represent Hawkes's long effort to overcome the repressive morality that triumphs in *The Owl* when the hangman's sympathy abates and the owl goes into flight, bringing down the less vigilant bird. The prisoner, who spiritually is the free man, is hung while the authority figure, the repressor who is essentially prisoner of his own repressed desire, survives. As early as *The Owl*, Hawkes recognized that love could not survive the legal/spiritual repression described earlier in terms of the owl digging into the female who had in effect trespassed on his emotions, a description which calls to mind the reptile on Catalina Kate's back in *Second Skin*: "The prowler, come perhaps to intercede for the prisoner, was caught by the owl, and, with fury and pointed ears, he sat upon her head, slowly raising and lowering his wings as a monk his cowl. He dug into her scalp, circumcising the brain. . .The owl labored and beat upon the woman, rasping through his gray hood. She tried to run, but he was fast to her and flapping, and the beat of his flooded wings slowed her" (*O*, p. 176).

The lesson is that the authority figure is ultimately the prisoner. But while Hawkes seems to have made this discovery as early as these two novellas, the protagonists of his subsequent novels struggle to achieve the sort of freedom that would make Michael Banks ride the horse of his desires rather than be destroyed by it.

Hawkes has called language "the best way to make intangibility concrete . . . It's the highest form of paradox—and I like paradox" (Kuehl, p. 176). Paradox in the early novellas and most of Hawkes's work triumphs and remains unresolved. While the hopefulness implied by the creative act balances and nullifies the darkness and horror of the landscape, the triumph of the hangman at the end of *The Owl* speaks to the role of History—the sense of past, social, and personal—whose repetitions Hawkes finds destructive in *The Cannibal*, yet whose destructive relentlessness Hawkes takes as creative inspiration throughout his work: "But I too believe in fiction—hard, ruthless, comic—and I myself believe very much in the sack of the past slung around our necks, in all the ancestral fears and abortive births we find in dreams as well as literature" (*Notes*

THE SACK OF THE PAST
THE CANNIBAL (1949)

"The world was shrouded in misery and blood and constituted a loathsome spectacle." (Charles Brockden Brown, *Wieland*)

At a time when oppressive reality seemed to dictate that imagination be superseded in war novels by an effort to *analyze* what had actually happened through graphic reconstruction, *The Cannibal* stood alone in American fiction as an imaginative art. Not content to produce another standard representation of war "as it really was," Hawkes uses the landscape and metaphors of war to seek out truths that extend past the horizontal approach to reality in which historical time is a calendar, and character, like landscape, remains regional and becomes dated. At age twenty-six, returning from ambulance duty in Italy and Germany, Hawkes seems to have been seeking a more satisfactory answer than that offered by conventional realists by employing exactly those means—a combination of the unconscious with historical time—that Olderman suggests in *Beyond the Wasteland* can shake our seemingly secure hold on reality: "If we glance back and forth from the abyss of the unconscious to the daily passage of historical time, we can easily lose hold on the whole idea of reality itself."

The reinterpretation of reality based on the inextricable link between historic time and the unconscious, the combination of which is the basic assumption of Hawkes's radical dualism, represents at the primary level of the creative writing a synthesis of seemingly polar forces within the writer, an ability to unleash the unconscious and manipulate the unknown that makes *The Cannibal* such a natural combination of instinct and art. Placed next to *Charivari*, *The Cannibal* represents a leap for Hawkes as a writer—from student to artist—and, to give credit where it is due, there is no doubt that Albert Guerard had a most positive influence on Hawkes at this important stage of his career, particularly in making Hawkes "aware of the distance between the writer and his materials and the idea of trying to maintain that distance . . . he was trying to help me to understand and to preserve the detachment." Hawkes cites this detachment as the key to his prose: "My writing depends on absolute detachment, and the unfamiliar or invented landscape helps me to achieve and maintain this detachment . . . I want to try to create a world, not represent it."

It was this distance and detachment, the keys to authorial control, which were missing from *Charivari*. Finding his natural intensity at the level of the microcosm (the sentence), and combining it with the distance necessary to maintain order in the larger structure, were the primary lessons Hawkes learned while writing *The Cannibal*. Perhaps the most mechanical and important change Hawkes made is suggested by this excerpt from an interview: "Hawkes: When I finished writing *The Cannibal*, *The Cannibal* was written in the third person. And when I finished it, I went through and changed all the pronouns to 'I'. Q: Zizendorf becoming . . .
Hawkes: A pseudo-narrator, which is what lends the narration that universality Albert Guerard speaks of in his introduction. I suddenly wanted to be in it myself" (*TREMA*, Paris III, p. 262).

There are two opposite yet not conflicting sensations which arise from *The*

Cannibal. One confronts at the sentence level a brilliant explosion of words that flows with the unconscious ease of automatic writing, yet represents a formidable labyrinth for the reader. At times, Hawkes's rhetorical structures seem to have almost an epic intention which, like Faulkner's, sweep the reader forward on the crest of the grand style: "To countenance the sickle over the wheat, to sweep out of the years the mellow heartbreak or the grand lie, to strike forward barehanded to a very particular and cold future, a diminutive but exact ending, a final satisfactory faith that is cruel and demonic, is to suffer the highest affection and lose it, to meet the loss of life and the advent of a certain reality" (*The C.*, p.201). The sound, as much as the meaning of the words, creates the impression of something grand yet terribly final. Like a swell at sea that rises into a wave, the sentence has to break, and where it does, the reader must focus attention. The technique lifts the reader and drops him where the fall, usually in the form of a single declarative sentence at the end of a paragraph, prepares one for the essential connection, the sentence which opens the new paragraph: "Madame Stella Snow combed her half-white, half-gold hair, hung her black gown from a hook on the wall and crawled into the bed . . . No drainpipes, chemicals to cleanse, flames to heat, no word, no food for the young or old, she was puzzled. Despite her years she could not find where it had all begun, for she was aristocratic to the end . . . She lay in the dark. Then she heard the scratching at the cellar door. All Germany revolved around Balamir . . ." (*The C* pp. 17-18).

Through *The Lime Twig*, Hawkes's detachment and control are accompanied at the sentence level by a great dependence on romance elements. In *The Cannibal*, a novel rather than a romance at the level of the superstructure, the essential verticality of a romance novel emerges brilliantly. Page 140 of *The Cannibal*, beginning with "My God, he's not coming at all!" to the end of the "Tonight" segment, "The light flared once and went out", is both a summation of the issues which precede it and an action which moves forward; but this "action" is not accomplished through the thoughts or actions of one character, but rather by a process which blends all characters into one, making all movement part of the unattended film Madame Snow's crippled son is projecting in the vast theatre. The verticality of the forward movement, most reminiscent of an orchestral score, is essential to the romance novelist's technique. The situation suggests elements of doubt, murder and oppression, as presented in the first stanza, " 'My God, he's not coming at all!' said Fegelein. 'Don't be a fool, it's almost time.' Sometimes I had to be harsh." and resolved in the final, "The light flared once and went out." The section in between should ideally be read as an orchestral score, that is, simultaneously as different parts which vary but move together to the same conclusion. Character, Time, and Space are on equal terms, listed by paragraphs whose first few words are sufficient to evoke a whole range of connections.

The romance techniques in *The Cannibal* are instinctual, if not unconscious, and exemplary. There are two ways in which the romance structure within the novelistic superstructure is woven. The first, essentially static, involves the "characters"; the second revolves around what can be loosely called Hawkes's symbolism. The essential difference between the two is that Hawkes, rejecting the novelistic notion of characters who create plot by moving forward through the fiction, and replacing them with figures who are either metaphors or pawns of Idea, allows his words what he will not allow his characters: growth. His characters are purposely one-dimensional, whereas the words which he loads vertically with meaning enjoy a far greater mobility than the figures whose flatness contributes to their essentially grotesque nature. Hawkes's characters remain prisoners; his words enjoy the freedom his characters cannot.

The characters in *The Cannibal* make clear the connection between Hawkes's romance figures, essentially metaphors rather than personalities, and the grotesque. People who can be defined by their role are grotesque, because, immobile in their attitudes, they are incapable of the vertical understanding and movement that make life more than a linear continuum. War is egalitarian in this sense. Sherwood Anderson's phrase, "They were all grotesques", applies equally to humanity. The cyclic form of *The Cannibal* takes the assumption even further. The grotesqueness of war is an ongoing condition. The Census Taker without a birth rate, the Signalman without a railroad, the Mayor who in the absence of order has no town to preside over, are reduced as individuals to their role in the power structure, clinging to their functions like Kafka's characters and offering absurd evidence in daily life of Sherwood Anderson's description: "And then the people came along. Each as he appeared snatched up one of the truths and some who were quite strong snatched up a dozen of them. It was the truths that made people grotesques . . . the moment one of the people took one of the truths to himself, called it a truth, and tried to live his life by it, he became a grotesque and the truth he embraced became a falsehood."

Zizendorf and Madame Snow are the only figures strong enough to play more than one role—Stella is a dance hall singer, a wife, a symbol of Germany: Zizendorf is an editor, a narrator, a murderer, an anarchist, and a politician—but they are as grotesque as Ernst or Balamir because both of them have recognized one truth and tried to live their life by it: Power. The irony in the utilization of such grotesques is that Hawkes in his later work is obsessed with uncovering and establishing what is the essential self. Skipper's problem in *Second Skin* stems from a reluctance, then a fear, to encounter this essential self. Mobility and vision are what finally make Skipper a survivor and a more novelistic character (though as "Skipper" he also functions as metaphor). In *The Cannibal*, only Zizendorf exhibits any distance—distance being the key both to his political power and narration.

In contrast, the building of image into symbol and metaphor is not concerned with establishing the static one-to-one relationship between image and idea that typifies allegory and is the basis for the essential grotesque nature of the characters. If image is properly cultivated into symbol or metaphor, then it is a mobile means of exploring abstracts that might be universal. Though it emerges as a character as important as Ernst or Balamir, the town, like the characters, remains essentially static, a symbol fixed as in allegory. Hawkes is at his best, his most mobile, when he finds either an image that can change as if through sensation—the lime—or an image which can mutate in the dark earth of the psyche. This is true of the dogs in *The Cannibal* and other works. The dogs are used as a metaphor for the unconscious warped into madness, and their development in *The Cannibal* is an example of Hawkes's technique at its best. One senses that the recurring images of the dogs grow from within, as if their development were not entirely planned, but seized upon by the author when the image was called for. This balance between the conscious and unconscious in the creation and development of symbolic patterns is reminiscent of the images of flight in Joyce's *Portrait*, images which never seem part of an imposed pattern, as do the images and metaphors of *Blood Oranges*, but are instead nonstatic images whose very meaning seems to have been discovered and developed while Joyce was deep in the process of writing. Just as Joyce was both conscious of the distance and control necessary to manipulate the images to their greatest effect, yet sufficiently "unconscious" to let them grow freely, Hawkes seems to have let his dogs appear and run without a leash while somehow always managing to keep them at his command and call.

The power of the dogs as metaphors is that, like the horse, Rock Castle, they can be either real or imaginary. They exist both in Ernst's subconscious and in his consciousness, they are both inside and outside the train compartment, they are both crazed dogs and passengers, and, as the distinction in the opening sentence implies, they are not mere symbols but real: "For unlike the monumental dogs found in the land of tumbleweed, glorified for their private melancholy and lazy high song, always seen resting on their haunches, resting and baying, these dogs ran with the train, nipped at the tie rods, snapped at the lantern from the caboose, and carrying on a conversation with the running wheels, begged to be let into the common parlor . . . As paying passengers they would eat and doze and leap finally back from the unguarded open platforms between cars into the night and the pack" (*The C*, pp. 95-6).

The dogs come to represent humanity in a state of mental and physical frenzy. Survival seems to depend on sexuality. Ernst is impotent, the dogs get the better of him; Gerta is "Lust," but her frenzied sexual efforts allow her, as the metaphor grows, the strength of company: "she had survived and hunted now with the pack" (*The C*, p. 101). As one of the human dogs, Gerta symbolizes the city: "her bright lopsided lips were red with the glistening static day of *das Grab*." The crazed "yipping" of the pack in *The Beetle Leg* is anticipated by this connection of the animal in the human with the image of the dog. The objectification of Ernst's inner torment precedes him as if it had existed always: "When she helped him down the iron steps . . . he knew things had changed, that the dogs had beaten them to their destination" (*The C*, p. 97); and at least part of the frenzy seems to involve jealousy—Cromwell has been making sexual overtones to Ernst's unlikely wife, Madame Snow. Hawkes's triumph is that the metaphor, born of Ernst's tortured imagination, has grown back from hallucination into reality: "The streets were as close as the sliding dark holds of a prison ship . . . provided little fare for the dogs that beat the train. They couldn't support the town dogs and certainly not these soldiers" (Ibid.).

Since the dog metaphor effectively comes to represent inner and outer realities, the unsteady rhythm of apocalypse and postwar realities, it is fitting that it be last used at the opening of the final section, "Land": "Madame Stella Snow's son, awakened by the barking of a dog . . ." (*The C*, p. 162). Madame Snow's son runs the movie theatre, the factory of dream as reality and reality as dream. Although the continued projections are in one sense meaningless because no one watches them, the repeated reference to the theatre creates the effect (which Pynchon later uses with such effectiveness as part of Slothrop's paranoia in *Gravity's Rainbow*) of history just possibly being a movie.

In the historically accurate, post-apocalyptic waste land of *The Cannibal*, the structures are, with the exception of Hawkes's novel itself, static and in decay. As Tony Tanner points out, both the mental institution and the institution for "higher learning", the University, are described as "menacing, piled backwards on itself in chaotic slumber". In *The Cannibal* almost all the major figures exist in the same structure, Madame Snow's house. Though Hawkes does not in *The Cannibal* overtly associate the House with Family and Security as he does from *The Beetle Leg* onwards, the fact that all the

21

characters live under the same roof and are dominated by the same mother figure inevitably suggests a family. The incestuous, claustrophobic unity is a microcosm of the town—the Census-Taker, Mayor, school teacher, and newspaper editor are all boarders; life, order, education, and communication are all part of this symbolic Germany. The use of Madame Snow's house prefigures the Banks/Hencher boarding house in *The Lime Twig*, both as a vertical romance structure, and, indirectly, as a symbol of security. If Madame Snow's house offers no security—the house breeds unhealthy sexuality (between Jutta, Madame Snow's sister, and Zizendorf) and eventually murder (first the school teacher, then the Mayor are disposed of in Zizendorf's takeover)—Madame Snow does make an effort to impose Order, which those susceptible to fascism seem to confuse with Security. She greets Balamir with more warmth than she shows her crippled son, telling the demented wanderer, "You're at home." But Balamir has reason to be wary—"Balamir knew he was not at home"—for in trying to maintain Order over the Chaos Balamir represents, Madame Snow tries to make the inmate from the mental institution a prisoner in her house: " 'Good night,' she said and turned the brass key" (*The C*, p. 7).

It is significant, therefore, that Zizendorf is a boarder in this structure, and emerges into the night from this microcosm of Germany. While Zizendorf's desire to liberate Germany, in many ways understandable, corresponds much more convincingly with his inner self than does Ernst's brief enactment of the Sarajevo assassination, Hawkes is careful to bring out the paradoxes. A new Germany needs to be born, but though Zizendorf is justified in feeling the Allied oppression, there is evidence in his essentially fascist treatment of his lover, Jutta, and her daughter, Selvaggia, that any "liberation" Zizendorf might be able to precipitate would effectively be a reimposition of Order, and as such a repetition of history. Zizendorf's comment at the end, "My order, the new campaign was planned and begun" (*The C*, p. 169), does not offer real hope for change; and the form of the novel, '45-'14-'45, suggests in metaphoric terms that Hitler was essentially a redefinition of the Kaiser.

This strange need in people to be governed by a Father (in part the meeting point between Fascism and the Roman Catholic Church) is not limited by Hawkes to Zizendorf's rise or to Germany. The example of the American colonel, who in preparation for the execution of the Priest "pulled forth his best garrison cap, polished the badge with a rag" and "busied himself with a worn grammar" (*The C*, p. 137), is nearly identical to that of the Mayor, who also has tremendous concern for detail; and while Zizendorf is more anarchistic in his approach while he is in the position of trying to obtain power, the connection is made in all three cases between Order and repression. Faced with a chaos with which the Church cannot cope, the new god is Order. As the school teacher, Stintz, explains to the colonel, "the war made a change in what a man might want to preach to the dumb people"; but though Nationalism is the new religion, the formidable opiate of the people, Order is shown to be the controlling metaphor. When Stintz says of the Priest, "I think maybe he did change", Zizendorf immediately responds, "He did not", for he understands that the essential connection between the "new gospel" and the old is Order. Both the political and religious establishments of Order are steeped in ceremony, the execution of the priest by the politicians, the substitution of one order for another, representing not only the formal union of the Colonel, Mayor, and Zizendorf, but a cannibalistic ritual.

Zizendorf's power seems to be based largely on his ability to control what the others, even Madame Snow, cannot: the madness of the situation. Zizendorf's understanding of and ability to recognize this metaphor of the times in others without succumbing to it represents a strength based to some degree on the fact that, like Hitler, Zizendorf contains the madness in himself. It is much the same madness as the Sheriff's in *The Beetle Leg*, but Zizendorf is less a prisoner of his self; he emerges as the "exceptional man". When Zizendorf goes with Jutta to the dance where Balamir and the other inmates are inextricably mixed with the townspeople, Jutta is described as looking like one of the "inmates" who "appeared with the same sackcloth idleness as Jutta". Only Zizendorf has the strength to leave the dance, his ability to pull Jutta out of the madness is indicative of the power he can exercise over people: "If I had left her for a moment and then returned, she would not have known who her partner was, but looking over shoulders that were all alike, she would have danced on" (*The C*, p. 33).

As narrator, Zizendorf's strength verges on the absolute strength of God or the Leader, a power established in the opening section of narration, "I thought it more appropriate to have my people keep their happiness and ideas of courage to themselves" (*The C*, p. 1). Furthermore, one of the men waiting with him for the appearance of the motorcycle asks, "But, my God, Leader, what can we do?"; and the apposition of God and Leader is as revealing as Zizendorf's dictatorial answer, "Don't think." His response inspires the murder of Stintz, the school teacher who is a potential rival for the young minds, just as the Mayor, also to be murdered, is a potential rival for the future Order. Though his role as narrator gives the Leader an almost god-like presence, as a human character rather than a metaphor, Zizendorf does exhibit a certain humanity: he is paranoid. The emergence of the Super Self, Zizendorf as Leader, is accompanied by the self-isolating paranoia of Hitler: "There was no one to trust" (*The C* p. 166).

The tie between narrative and political manipulation, at first expressed as Zizendorf's "need to recreate" (*The C*, p. 23), is skillfully reprised towards the end: "I, the Leader, the compositor, put the characters, the words of the new voice, into the stick" (*The C*, p. 175). Typical of such a leader and narrator, Zizendorf's personal repressiveness has the final word, and it augurs another wave of repression for the new generation. Jutta's daughter, Selvaggia, "wild-eyed from watching the night and the birth of the Nation", ironically asks, " 'What's the matter, Mother? Has anything happened?' I answered instead of Jutta, without looking up, and my voice was vague and harsh; 'Nothing. Draw those blinds and go back to sleep . . . ' She did as she was told" (*The C*, p. 195).

The first section of the 1945 narration ends with Zizendorf, who describes himself as Madame Snow's "lover", waiting in the cold to murder and capture the symbol of potency, the American overseer's motor-bike. Part Two, 1914, is divided into seven subsections—*Love, Stella, Ernst, Lust, Tonight, Leader, Land*. The transition from Zizendorf's narration, in which it becomes clear that war is the perversion of love, to the first segment, entitled *Love*, is skillful. This cut to the past, coupled with the heading *Love*, suggests Eden, a symbol of possibilities in the past that are unreachable in the present. Typically, Hawkes rejects easy nostalgia. The description of young Stella, already the Image, contains a backdrop of flowers, but the idyll is already very much Eden on the verge of the fall. The scene is a sport club's beer hall, and Stella, like Dietrich in "Blue Angel", is being paid to be romantic.

Hawkes makes clear that the Image is dangerous in terms of Love as well as politics. Ernie, the Brauhaus owner's grotesque, claw-handed son (his physical deformity signals the inner limitation which makes him a "grotesque"), falls in love not with Stella but with her voice, an early indication in Hawkes's work of the dangerous power of the Image, both as the basis of romantic love (of which Hugh in *The Blood Oranges* is a similar victim), and the sort of political demagoguery that Hitler's voice inspired. Ernst is the perfect victim because, being a romantic and a Christian, he believes in the Image. He accuses Stella, after the death of her mother which allows her to stay in her father's room until he dies, of not doing penance before the image: " 'You don't even have a cross,' he said" (*The C*, p. 36). Like Hugh, Ernst is incapable of actual human love because he is overly spiritual and Christian. In words that speak to the dangers of elitism both in art and religion, Ernst believes that "The upper world was superior." The position suggested by this line is in conflict with the fact that, appearing later as Gavrillo Princip, Ernst/Princip is supposed to have destroyed what in social terms was the "upper world." Like the photographer Hugh in *The Blood Oranges*, Ernst's relationship to the Image suggests a total lack of the distance necessary for an artist towards his work or a man from his self: "He walked up and down the room, could see nothing from the window because he was too near the light" (*The C*, p. 91). There is no surprise that the "love" between Ernst and Stella is doomed. Their love flares briefly when Stella suddenly feels terribly alone—love becoming the extinguisher of fear— but Ernst is essentially too preoccupied with his absurd figures, symbols of Christ's example of pain as the result of a love too spiritual to allow a healthy human response. Ernst continues to carve wooden Christs, comes to see himself as a martyr, and not surprisingly is crucified by the experience of life.

It is also not surprising that the segment called "love" is about the perversion of what is most natural. Stella is first seen moving "as if she had a sunflower just beneath her bosom," but whatever innocence she may have had is quickly absorbed by the crowd: "losing one by one those traits that were hers, absorbed more and more the tradition that belonged to all. She did not lisp when she sang, but boomed the words in an unnatural voice" (*The C*, p. 45). Reminiscent of the townspeople's attitude to Hester in *The Scarlet Letter*, Stella's power of beauty is transformed into the power of evil. She is described first as a "sorceress"; and then, in language strikingly reminiscent of Hawthorne's association of witch, "black man," and wilderness in *The Scarlet Letter*, Hawkes connects her power with the devil, "the devil had come a long way from the forest to find her" (*The C*, p. 45). Like Hester, Stella carries an ignominious seal—"Every dress she owned was stamped with the seal of the campfollower"—but what was largely repression in *The Scarlet Letter* has been brought up to date in *The Cannibal*: the wasteland has come so far from Eden that guilt, like love, is meaningless; the seal represents society's approval, not its disgrace.

The repressiveness associated with love, the apparent personal enjoyment of the pain the world was to feel—"Beneath her eyes she had painted indigo stains as if she had been beaten" (*The C*, p. 45)—is what links the sexual in *The Cannibal* with the political. In understanding Hawkes's use of the political/ sexual metaphor, it should be remembered that at least up until *The Blood Oranges* and possibly the trilogy, Hawkes depicts love as an irresolvable choice between sexuality and comfort, an antagonism which may explain why his depiction of sexuality is largely without sensuality or tenderness. The killing of the American overseer for the symbol of his power has vaguely homosexual overtones, "I'll get him in the behind—behind" (*The C*, p. 143). In both sexual and political action the perversion of Germany becomes self-willed, self-propagating. Madame Snow, who as Image is the symbol of both sexual and political power, emerges as "the very hangman, the eater, the greatest leader of us all." That this "hangman," recalling "Il Gufo" in *The Owl*, is also "the eater" suggests Stella's role as cannibal. She participates with the Duke in eating her nephew. The eating process by which cannibalism becomes the metaphor for human life consumed by war is given its most striking dramatization in the scene (pp. 180-2) in which the Duke hunts, dismembers, and eats Jutta's son. The deranged Duke believes that the boy is a fox, and after the capture, the Duke's clumsiness in the dissection of the youth is painful to the point that the reader must either laugh or scream.

The political implications of the hostile male/female relationship that has Ernst "eaten" by Stella and Jutta by Zizendorf; and the horrible sexual battle between the American overseer, Leevey, and the German whore, are perhaps raised most powerfully by the attack Madame Snow and her group of women launch to control the inmates of the mental institution. Though there is sufficient madness in the air for one to accept the monkeys imitating Shakespeare— "Dark is life, dark, dark is death" (*The C*, p. 143)—one must wonder at first why the women attack the institution. The answer seems to be that the opposition between forces which are essentially the masses of the disenfranchised— women and those deemed abnormal by those in control of society—is exactly what the "Director" wants. Though in his later work there is an absence of such overt social concern, young Hawkes, like Kafka, seems to have been disturbed by the relationship between power and control: "From a fourth floor window, the Director, wrapped in a camel's hair coat, watched the struggle until he saw the woman, led by Stella, rush the ridiculous inmates; he drew the blinds and returned to his enormous files" (*The C*, p. 156).

The Director is the ultimate cannibal, for it is he who controls the Institution, and he who most blatantly denigrates Man. When the riot has been quelled, "the Director finally issued an order for the burial of the animals." Even Zizendorf is conscious that *men* are involved, "some twenty or thirty dead men were left, and they never disappeared."

The meaning of the title should not be overlooked, nor should it be limited to the obvious grotesque action of postwar Europe, in which survival became an exaggerated continuation of the basic consumer process of capitalism. The relevance to contemporary American life that the title suggests is profound. The relationship between consumer technocracy and everyday personal interaction is inevitable and devastating. Zizendorf's cannibalistic relationship with Jutta—he consumes her love, he uses her with indifference—is no more German than it is American. The lasting significance of *The Cannibal* derives from the evidence that war merely exaggerates the process by which humans are reduced to a commodity, making emotions something that can be consumed.

In the brief section of narration which precedes the three major sections in *The Cannibal*, the narrator describes the novel's town as an Eden, a coveted Image of something past that lives in the present as memory: "It is a garden spot: all our memories are there, and people continually seek it out." Recalling Olderman's statement that what differentiates the romance novel of the 1960s from its predecessors is the shift in the "controlling metaphor" from a sense of a "lost Eden" to "the image of a wasteland," Hawkes would seem to emerge as the transition figure to what has become the predominant assumption in American literature: that life is a battle with the growing wasteland. For the American writers up through the 1950s, Eden and innocence represented a nostalgia for the idea of a lost paradise. *The Cannibal* and *The Beetle Leg*, on the other hand, both suggest that the resulting sense of loss may be based on a nostalgia for something that never existed.

FROM FISHING ROD TO LIGHTHOUSE
THE BEETLE LEG (1951) and *SECOND SKIN* (1964)

"For me the writer should always serve as his own angleworm—and the sharper the barb with which he fishes himself out of the blackness, the better."
(John Hawkes, *Notes On The Wild Goose Chase*)

In many respects *The Beetle Leg* and *Second Skin* represent opposite sides of Hawkes's fiction. *The Beetle Leg* is an extension of the nightmarish wasteland of *The Cannibal*, the title suggesting the arid landscape that grows from the sexual repression of the earlier book into the moraltiy which the Sheriff would use to maintain law and order. *Second Skin*, on the other hand, is an effort actually to overcome the puritan morality that pervades Hawkes's early work. In *Second Skin*, Skipper sets out from the bus terminal with his daughter, Cassandra, his granddaughter, Pixie, and a bus load of soldiers. This "point of departure" represents the beginning of a voyage away from the wasteland of Skipper's past, including his death-oriented youth (his father, an undertaker, is not dissuaded from suicide by young Skipper's cello, just as Adeppi's voice is squashed in *Goose on the Grave*), and, most immediately, the war in the Pacific where he was a naval captain.

Technically, Skipper's first person narration is the most striking difference between the novels, and Skipper's ability to construct (or reconstruct) his life from the island of his imagination is a metaphor for the hopefulness implied by his story. In *The Beetle Leg*, the opening piece of the Sheriff's narration, balanced by Cap Leech's brief monologue at the end, suggests a closed prison—there is little mobility in the act of narration, and no mobility in the sense of self-awareness or understanding on the part of the grotesquely flat characters. While Skipper's first person narration represents a shift towards more standard narrative fiction, it is an effort—as much on the part of the author as his narrator—to come to terms with the waste land that is always an inner as well as an external landscape. In *The Lime Twig*, the experience of Michael Banks with Rock Castle, the horse of his subconscious, suggests that the individual must not only release the natural forces of desire, but also confront and understand the subterranean forces. Skipper experiences, in a voyage of the self that speaks to the novel's strangely picaresque quality, all the horror of repressed sexuality that Banks feels. Skipper is Hawkes's first novelistic narrator, and the first capable of reasoning and eventually of understanding. Unreliable to the point where his own perceptions are faulty (he fails, for example, to recognize his feelings for his daughter Cassandra), Skipper's first person narration is in direct contrast to Banks, who never escapes the prison of third person narration in which the characters in *The Beetle Leg* also are confined. The waste land of *The Beetle Leg* is the puritanical New England island that Skipper must confront before he is able to find the second, more idyllic island in the sun. Hawkes said in 1962: "For me the writer should always serve as his own angleworm—

and the sharper the barb with which he fishes himself out of the blackness, the better." The fishing metaphor he uses just prior to the publication of *Second Skin* is the same that he used to such effect in *The Beetle Leg*.

The real importance of the fishing metaphor, both in terms of *The Beetle Leg* and Hawkes's later novels, is that it suggests the bringing to the surface of something which, in the case of the dead baby, may be horrible, or, in Camper's desire to "go fishing", something closer to Banks's horse, that side of man which releases desire in opposition to security and reason. Certainly the voyages of metaphoric self-discovery that Skipper (and to a lesser extent, Allert in *Death, Sleep and the Traveler*) undergo depend on just such a process of reeling in what lies beneath the surface of the subconscious. The fishing metaphor thus speaks to Hawkes's overall creative process. Hawkes, like Cap Leech, who delivers Bohn from the womb of his dead mother—"The son, fished none too soon from the dark hollows, swayed coldly to and fro between his fingers" ·(*BL*, p. 121)—succeeds in going beneath the surface to produce from the unknown something which resembles life. The pain that resounds in *Second Skin* in the scene at the outset where Skipper is tattooed in green with the name of his daughter's dead, homosexual husband, signals that consciousness, like memory, involves the voyager in peeling back the surface to get at the second skin.

In *The Beetle Leg*, although the characters themselves remain unaware, what lies beneath the surface in conflict. *The Beetle Leg* belongs to a select group of American novels (*The Scarlet Letter* and *Go Down Moses*, for example) which succeed not only in delineating and dramatizing the roots of American conflict, but take on mythic proportions that transcend the local, the American, and raise the work to the level of universal truth.

The landscape of *The Beetle Leg* is a waste land of epic proportions—"the Slide . . . was like a whole corner of the world fell in" (*BL*, p. 26)—and though Hawkes's unnostalgic depiction of the American west is clearly Eden after the Fall and the Flood—"The first man had died in Eden, they pronounced him dead. And now, with brightening eye, he found himself sitting in the middle of the washed-out garden's open hearth" (*BL*, p. 140)—Hawkes, who again functions as God over his narrators, does not equate original sin with sexuality. Rather, the disaster seems to be the natural result of the unhappy union between near-Olympian forces (the wilderness and the powers that would control it), a combination which results ultimately in the sterile morality of the inhabitants.

Although by *Second Skin* Hawkes seems concerned with finding a state of functional harmony, *The Beetle Leg*, while not as ripe with paradox as *The Lime Twig*, is sustained by the conflict of paradoxical opposites—Nature and Technology, Fire and Water, Man and Woman, Conscious and Subconscious. The book suggests, where these apparently polar forces intersect, American life hangs in the balance. Just as the scaffold, the jail, and the forest are built into the archetypal romance structures of *The Scarlet Letter*, the figures on the horizon of *The Beetle Leg*—and there is no essential difference between jail, dogs, mountain, river, dam, and the characters—are drawn to mythic proportions. The overriding conflict that both characters and landscape share is between Freedom (associated with the wilderness, the desert, the river, certain women, the area between consciousness and the unconscious, the dogs, and the Red Devils) and Control (linked to the Sheriff, his jail, the dam, business, government, and impotent men). ·

In this conflict there is only one survivor, one person who can cross the boundaries between the absolutes of Wilderness and Control—and he is mad. A force somehow above wilderness and technology, Cap Leech is able to move over the vast waste land with relative impunity. In contrast to Leech's red wagon and suggestive of the lack of mobility that makes the Sheriff his own prisoner, the Jail is set on the border between Town (civilization, control) and the Wilderness (the desert), an area outside the law, just as it was outside the circle of the settlement's morality in *The Scarlet Letter*. As with Zizendorf and the hangman/narrator of *The Owl*, the example of the Sheriff suggests that the corollary to power is fear. Though the Sheriff's jurisdiction ends where nature takes over (he is unable to arrest the semi-nude man "snarled with this river" [*BL*, p. 13]), the relationship in *The Beetle Leg* between morality and law is as strong and repressive as it is in Hawthorne's novel. In his opening section, the Sheriff sees the desert and the river as threats associated with the unknown and sexuality; and because sexuality involves passion which cannot always be controlled, the Sheriff would regulate sexuality with laws, just as the government and construction company would dam up the river. Significantly, the first town to survive in the waste land Hawkes calls Gov. City, signalling the relationship between Government, whose laws set limits on nature, define morality, and otherwise establish Control, and City, which physically defines space, often with the imposition of a highly ordered grid, a connection fundamental to understanding the emergence of modern America.

In the section that immediately follows the description of the origins of Government City, Town is associated in the minds of both Camper and his wife, who are lost in the desert, with Security, that is, what is known and conscious. The inner fear of Lou, Camper's wife, that "There isn't any town out here" (*BL*, p. 49), is based on a profound need for security which will keep her a prisoner of the House for the rest of the novel (just as Margaret Banks will be), and causes her to urge Camper to "Take us back to the highway", the man-made transition between the Wilderness and Town.

The Great Slide represents the momentary triumph of the Wilderness (water) over Technology (the dam). The dam represents not only man's control over Water and its association with women and sexuality—"the river rose . . . the women came" (*BL*, p. 48)—but it represents the people's misplaced faith in government and technology. "It held. They told the visitors it would" (*BL*, p. 68). But the dam *doesn't* hold, and it is through this disaster that Hawkes's implicit criticism of government is at its most exacting. There is no sense that the flood is retribution for sexuality; on the contrary, it represents the triumph of the forces of natural freedom which are in opposition to Home: "The water lay above the roof tops" (*BL*, p. 133).

While the Great Slide does not resolve the essential conflicts, the description of the "sarcophagus of mud" easing "down the rotting shale a beetle's leg each several anniversaries" (*BL*, pp. 67-8) is a fine example of Hawkes's talents, for it conveys a sense of timelessness and verticality of meaning—a natural disaster, a symptom of the disease of the Metal and Lumber Company, which sees it first in loss of tools and only coincidentally in loss of life—that contribute to the mythical quality of the dead man, Mulge Lampson. Mulge's is the archetypal death—"There was one death" (*BL*, p. 7), "there's just one man who died out there" (*BL*, p. 45)—and the association of his grave with the mountain ("The mile long knoll of his grave was an incomplete mountain" [*BL*, p. 66]) builds to the point that he becomes one with the mountain, another Christ figure. But Hawkes rejects the easy symbolism, and Mulge's death is turned into a product which plays on the American nostalgia for death—"His razor was spread open before the shaving mug on a square of Christmas paper . . . for fifty cents the relics could be touched." While Mulge is *remembered* as a Christ figure ("In those days you could have followed him down the street . . . And if he stopped you could have touched him"), in fact he is nothing more than a technological cowboy ("And as far as going into the field or prairie, not him . . . But he went on the project . . . worked with machinery that could chew a man to pieces" [*BL*, p. 100]).

The Beetle Leg starts with institutional madness, the Sheriff's first person narrative, and ends with Cap Leech's short piece of first person narrative, a suggestion of the triumph of a madness that is outside the law, but still present in nature. Cap Leech, who has lost his licence to practice medicine, is medicine man to the Indians, riding over the unknown landscape at night pulled by "Pegasus of a branded species", a "mad horse" which hauls Leech and wagon into the sky as the Sheriff flees; his own brand of animal madness is amply demonstrated by his march around the barnyard and the mutilation of the rooster, a scene reminiscent of the Duke's cannibalism. This is typical of Hawkes's depiction of life as paradox; to understand Cap Leech, one must first understand the Sheriff.

The first clue to the Sheriff's ultimate loss of power is his portrayal as a reader—"He stopped reading, marked his place and began to talk" (*BL*, p. 10). The Sheriff's reading of almanacs and astronomy suggests a chink in his personal armament; though authoritarian, the Sheriff is not as "authorial" as Leech is. While Leech can deliver horror and accept it with a terrible creative distance (the extraction of Bohn from his dead mother's womb), the Sheriff's chief goal is to control the unknown as he would control everything else in the universe. The Sheriff's reading does not represent enquiry as a means to understanding; rather, it is a reflection of his need for Order which the medicine man's essential amorality upsets. In contrast to the amorality of the medicine man, the Sheriff's moral law is self-confining; he believes in the Town—"A man is wise if he keeps to town" (*BL*, p. 10)—and its corollaries, Home, Family, and Security, which Hawkes finds suspect. The basis of the Sheriff's need for this Order is fear of the journey into the self that Michael Banks and Skipper will undergo: "A man's eyes burn, he ain't too comfortable when he has got to stand in front of his own cell door, to stare at the one who is now inside . . . " (*BL*, p. 9).

As "The one who is now inside" suggests, the characters in *The Beetle Leg* work in pairs or doubles (Sheriff and his Deputy Wade; Bohn and his whipping boy, Finn, the ex-bronc rider); in each instance the lesser figure serves as a subconscious that the more powerful figure abuses or suppresses. The implication that the Sheriff and his deputy are different sides of the same self is carefully developed: "In the jail office they did not face each other, rather they waited side by side, the Sheriff's hand on the other's arm . . . " (*BL*, p. 31). Whenever the mission threatens the Sheriff's ordered world (for instance, whenever Cap Leech is involved), the Sheriff sends Deputy Wade out into the night.

The basic impotence of the Sheriff's moral law is contained in his view of women either as whores or mothers. No female is allowed to enter his cell, the jail of his mind—"And there's one thing sure; it'll never have to hold no woman. There are other rooms in town for that" (*BL*, p. 8)—because sexuality threatens the order of his universe. What the Sheriff requires, troubled as he is with the external manifestations of his inner fears (the Red Devils), is surface stability, as suggested by his reference to the jail as a faithful woman: "She don't change" (*BL*, p. 33).

While the Sheriff is the ultimate moral/legal authority—"The Clare Sheriff was invested with the office to inspect, whip or detain any descendant of the Fork country pale families, was in a position to remember when they settled and how well or poorly they had grown" (*BL*, p. 42)—Cap Leech, who wears "ministerial strings", rules over the world of the unconscious and sex. Encountered by Deputy Wade while symbolically raping a young Indian by extracting a tooth, Leech's domination of the Sheriff is signalled by his association with the river and the mobility of his red wagon which takes him "to the limits" of experience, linking him to Indians and fire—"Now and then a volley of firecrackers burst from a huddle of black-braided Indians and with a dismal but high pitched cry they scattered, then returned panting toward the wagon" (*BL*, p. 35). Leech's "housewagon", "a small fortress of unmatched parts," is in obvious opposition to the fixity of the Sheriff's jail; and this opposition, clearly sexual in nature (the medicine-man works in the back of a wagon depicted as a large red hole), is something that must be encountered and cannot be bypassed—when Wade comes across the red wagon, "It had not been driven to the side but blocked the road" (*BL*, p. 37).

The meeting between the Sheriff and Leech is essential to the understanding of the two opposing views in *The Beetle Leg*—the Sheriff's, with his concern for astrology representing a mad, fearful, strangely Faustian belief in Order; and the medicine-man's, his can of ether suggesting his dominance over dreams and the unconscious, representing an amoral, satanic position, the basis of which is the assumption the Sheriff mouths but would refute; "It is a lawless country." The evidence of their encounters is the depiction of the medicine-man as a black magician—"With one stroke, a cupping of the wand hand, he could withdraw the rooster's coiled meld while it died vertically on the wall" (*BL*, p. 151)—his powers push the Sheriff past the limits of Control.

It is at the point where the Sheriff must confront Leech, where in a sense he confronts himself, that the image of the dog, which in *Charivari* was associated with the grey space separating Henry from Emily, and which in *The Cannibal* was the exteriorization of Ernst's madness, is invoked. As Leech enters the jail, "Behind, on the streets they had just left, the loping body of a wild dog appeared at the cloudless, hardly sleeping skyline, turned and bounded into the jail" (*BL*, p. 40). The Sheriff instinctively is put on the defensive, consulting his zodiacal almanac: "A gambled harvest, the weather, and days on which accidents were most likely to occur, he calculated" (*BL*, p. 41). Momentarily reassured, he tells Wade to "go bring me that pointing dog," but the control and obedience that a pointing dog implies is short-lived, for there is something sexual in the nature of the contact between the two powers: "The Sheriff stretched forth a palm like a large gland, then Leech; and they shook hands" (Ibid.).

Leech with his can of ether has the better of this show of power, for he recognizes what lies beneath the surface of the waste land: disease. Indeed, what frightens the Sheriff to the point that he calls back the defense of his subconscious ("Wade . . . come here, Wade!"), is that Leech suggests that the Sheriff himself represents in Clare the juncture between disease and the self: Leech examines the Sheriff's palm and "drew a circle with his broken fingertip.

'Disease,' he said, 'thriving. Catch a fly in your fist and you could infect the town.' Quickly with the iced cotton, he swabbed the hand, let it go. 'Clean. For awhile' " (*BL*, p. 43). This metaphor of recurring disease is essential to understanding the process of Hawkes's work, for what lies beneath the surface in the individual inevitably reappears in his actions, personal or political; and, as the form of *The Cannibal* suggested, history recurs like disease.

The relationship between the dogs and the Red Devils, who attack the pointer (the symbol of the dog under control), demonstrates the intricate symbolic weave which both moves the action of the novel forward and unifies it structurally. The first mention of the Red Devils immediately follows the first invocation of the dogs; as the novel spins forward, the dogs and the Red Devils become inextricably linked as symbols of inner disorder, symbolic inhabitants of that "grey area" that speaks to a disequilibrium between conscious and unconscious states verging in its intensity on madness. The Red Devils, described as "jerkined Indians", are not only in conflict with the Town's legal order—"License plates had been stripped from the mudguards" (*BL*, p. 24)—but are responsible symbolically for moral chaos. After they leave town for the first time, "it was impossible to tell which were men and which women," a distinction fundamental to the Sheriff's sense of moral order. Indicative of the romance weave, the threats to order reappear, accompanied by the dogs: "At that moment one Red Devil . . . looked over his shoulder toward the trailing dogs . . . Behind him the scampering dogs . . . drew near with forced cries and shaggy heads, bewildered in the sudden opportunity to run. With each crafty burst of the engine, the barks, a sound hoarse and long unheard, started anew" (*BL*, pp. 104-5).

The effect of the ties between Red Devils and dogs, connected as they are with the Sheriff, is not only of a tight romance structure but a mobility of symbols, a virtual interchangeability capable, as when the Red Devils are associated with fire at the end of the novel ("its rider fled, turned to flame under the little seat, reared, contorted into a snake embrace, and fell writhing in fire" [*BL*, p. 157]), of making a whole range of metaphoric connections within the metaphoric domain of the Wilderness: dogs—Red Devils—unconscious—horses—Red Wagon—Cap Leech—fire—Indians—sexuality—pain.

The Red Devils' association with fire is of further interest because Ma, an Indian girl who lives with Luke Lampson (the brother of Ma's ex-husband, the mythical Mulge), is also connected with this image. The Mandan refers to Ma as "the stove woman," and her "deep skillet" suggests not only the comfort associated with warmth, the womb, and food, but also the grotesqueness of daily life inherent in repetition, the unchanged cooking fat. The fire of Ma's stove is the transition symbol between Cap Leech's wilderness fire, a blaze which verges on madness, and the Town—Luke "had bargained for Ma's stove in a vacant barn *on the edge of Clare*" (*BL*, p. 97)—and is the connecting symbol between the two apparently polar natural forces, fire and water, which in *The Beetle Leg* both originate in women.

Ma's fire, though lit in terms of Comfort, is effectively out in terms of sexuality, doused as it were by the Mandan's water. Like the Sheriff, Ma has a mysterious disease—"no one knew how the sore had begun on her arm" (*BL*, p. 65)—whose recurrence recalls the metaphoric rising to the surface of the Sheriff's disease. At the surface level of her dialogue, Ma's repressiveness is typical of an essentially puritanical American rural morality: "You don't watch me now! This finery ain't for men to see—except in the dark" (*BL*, p. 79).

This repressed sexuality finds expression in Ma's jealousy of Luke over the Mandan, the irony being that Luke is essentially asexual: it is Luke who kills the snake for the Campers; he is also referred to as "snake-killer" by Camper on their late night fishing expedition.

The symbolic opposition of Ma's fire (Comfort) and the Mandan's water (potential sexuality) represents the space that separates Camper and his wife; and this broad grey patch of darkness associated with the mad dogs seems to come between man and woman in every marital relationship that Hawkes portrays, with the exception of Skipper and Catalina Kate, and Cyril and Fiona. Henry and Emily, Ernst and Stella, Camper and Lou, Michael and Margaret Banks, Hugh and Catherine, Miranda and Skipper, Allert and Ursula, as well as the unnamed narrator of *Travesty* and his wife Honorine, all suffer from an inability to resolve the instinct for Comfort with the drive for sexuality, a tension that threatens the institution of marriage, particularly where Christian morality and the law intersect in Fidelity. The equation of Woman with Comfort and Man with sexual drive is not, however, as cut and dry as it might first appear. Though Hawkes is writing about a world in which the male traditionally has more mobility than the female, Hawkes's females all exhibit a sexual drive, though, with the exception of Stella, Fiona and Ursula, it is secondary to their role as Comforter for their men. In the cases of Emily, Lou, Margaret, and Catherine, repression distorts the woman's desires. Lou's sexuality exists just as strongly as Camper's, but her fantasy is perverted by repression: Lou hallucinates a monstrous Red Devil at her window in much the same way that Margaret Banks creates Thick, her abuser, out of her sexual frustrations.

The problem is easier to delineate than to resolve. When Luke Lampson first comes upon the Campers stranded in the sands of the wasteland, the headlights of their car are illuminating a sign which captions their problem, reflecting upon the problem of all Hawkesian marriages: "POISON WATER" (*BL*, p. 25). In other words, what is natural between man and woman, the sexuality implied by water, has somehow been polluted.

Camper, a grotesque, is, in spite of his assertion "I'm a hunter . . . You took me for a tourist" (*BL*, p. 97), a tourist to the wilderness. Leaving Lou behind is part of the particular American myth that sexuality and strength are rejuvenated not with women but in contact with other men and nature. Hawkes shatters this nostalgic myth by showing how the madness of such a journey finally sends Camper running home to Lou. Thus, while Camper has a sexual drive as insatiable as water itself—" 'I couldn't keep away from it' he said, ' . . .I had to see it' " (*BL*, p. 96)—and while the image of a fisherman dipping his rod into the water is carefully built into a sexually symbolic action, Hawkes recognizes the sterility of the act: the men catch only a dead baby.

The men's fishing boat sinks back into the water of the subconscious, the lake created by the natural disaster; and the stage is set for Cap Leech's final moments of triumphant madness. The defeat of the Sheriff by Cap Leech represents the triumph of magic over morality. But what is this magic? Leech, "the Missouri madman", walks the fine line between American pragmatism ("Her only discoloration was for a purpose, and Cap Leech believed in the non-usefulness of burst organs; no good could come from it" [*BL*, p. 122]) and cruelty (the mad, ritualistic execution of the rooster). Essentially neuter, Leech's power, his magic and his madness, is based on an extreme form of pragmatism. There are only the natural forces of this earth, and these are neither good nor evil, because for Leech, reality is powerful, contradictory, and cruel. The fact that Leech has the final word suggests that the wasteland of *The Cannibal* continues. It is this nightmare reality, struggled with but not overcome by Michael Banks in *The Lime Twig* that is the point of departure for Skipper's voyage of the self in *Second Skin*.

The shift in the role of the narrative voice that one sees between *The Beetle Leg* and *Second Skin* represents a realization that the individual must for the sake of survival take responsibility for his "self," thereby taking control of his fate. Prior to Banks's desperate run, this had always been severely imposed by the author through authoritarian figures and a control over the narrative voice that never allowed his token first person narrators the mobility of reason. Hawkes recognizes the implications of this shift to a more conventional first person voice: "Of course it's obvious that from *The Cannibal* to *Second Skin* I've moved from nearly pure vision to a kind of work that appears to resemble much more closely the conventional novel. In a sense there was no other direction to take." This shift away from the "pure vision" of romance towards the novel proper seems to be the result of Hawkes's interest, encouraged by Guerard, in the possibilities of first person narration. This is not to suggest that Hawkes loses his authorial detachment. When Skipper is tattooed at the outset of *Second Skin*, the reader winces with him, proof of Hawkes's creative axiom that "the product of extreme fictive detachment is extreme fictive sympathy." As Donald Greiner points out, the remarkable thing about Hawkes's authorial detachment is that it frees the reader to sympathize with characters who otherwise would merely disgust us; the sympathy, for instance, one feels not for Luke, but for what is supposed to have preceded the waste land—Innocence—when Luke fishes the dead baby out of the reservoir.

Hawkes does, however, speak of "rarifying" the roles and rhetoric of his first person narrators: "I think that there is a really clear progression from Hencher in *The Lime Twig* to Skipper, then to Cyril, and then to Allert. The progression's sort of going from Hencher, becoming much more elaborate and hysterical almost with Skipper and the very rich hysteria of Skipper becoming a little more refined and much more lyrical with Cyril. Cyril's voice getting muffled and much more somber in Allert's voice" (*TREMA*, Paris III, p. 261).

Skipper's "hysterical" narration is inextricably linked to the problems of his "self." Indeed there is the sense that Skipper's problem is a narrative problem, a problem of distance and perception; for consciousness, the growing ability to perceive, is both what distinguishes Skipper from the early narrators, and gives him the chance to overcome his impotence, part of the waste land that still lingers in *Second Skin*. Although Skipper fails with his daughter Cassandra, he succeeds finally in showing himself the "true tonality of the thing"; by experiencing the events for a second time as narrator, he is able to put them into perspective and survive.

Skipper's survival, a harmony created out of the conflict of paradoxical forces (father as son—"Skipper . . . don't be a child, please" [*SS*, p. 15], male as female, "I would not have matured into a muscular and self-willed Clytemnestra but rather into a large and innocent Iphigenia" [*SS*, p. 1]), is no small feat, for it represents man's coming to peace with his self and Time, a harmony that Cassandra, described in conflict ("old-young", "schizophrenic"), never achieves. Prefiguring Cyril's struggle with Hugh, the love that emerges from Skipper's struggle with his self is repeatedly an assertion of life over death: "Perhaps my father thought that by shooting off the top of his head he would force me to undergo some sort of transformation. But, poor man, he forgot my capacity for love" (*SS*, p. 2). This life force inside Skipper leads to his rebirth but it is discovered only after a voyage that suggests many of the obstacles to harmony are generated from within.

Skipper's journey takes him cross country in a Greyhound bus and over water to his islands, but his voyage of self-discovery is unlike almost any other in American literature (with the possible exception of the trials of the hero of Barth's *The Sot Weed Factor*). The process by which the protagonist assimilates his trials is handled in terms of implicit metaphoric implication, the irony of authorial detachment reflected in Skipper's comic impotence and imperception. Hawkes cites Skipper's lack of perception (symbolically dramatized by his belated arrival at the lighthouse) as the key to Skipper's unreliability: "The extent to which he is unaware of his powerful relationship to his daughter is one way we could think of Skipper as an imperceptive narrator" (Kuehl, p. 116). Skipper is disappointed when Cassandra shows "No appetite . . . No desire" when he offers her a sandwich, and he fails to recognize the source of his own hunger. Shortly before the bus splits in two, Skipper comments, "I felt that I knew myself, heart and stomach, a peaceful father of my own beautiful and unpredictable child, and that the disheveled traveler was safe, that both of us were safe" (*SS*, p. 34).

On one level, the bus trip is about the forces of the subconscious. The symbolic thrust of the action stretches plausibility: though they are "sailing out, I could feel, in a seventy-eight-mile-an-hour dive into the thick of night," they are unharmed, and land "standing still. We were upright" (*SS*, p. 34). Father and daughter are stranded on the same lonesome highway as husband and wife Camper, and the sexual nature of the trip can be further seen in both the description of the highway as "a dead snake in the distance" (*SS*, p. 35), and in the behaviour of the three AWOL sailors (outside of the law, their sexuality is in conflict with the father's sense of security through order), who are described as "three deadly lizards", threateningly sexual reptiles who prefigure the reptilian "monster" on Catalina Kate's back. These "three small soldiers" are "three black silhouettes" (*SS*, p. 39) who fight in the war for Skipper's psyche. Though they may also be a real threat in terms of the barely demonstrable surface reality of the scene, they emerge after Skipper has repressed the threatening memory of Tremlow: "gritting my teeth at that silent chaos, the myriad notes of the unconsciousness, I found myself thinking of Tremlow, once more saw him as he looked when he bore down upon me during the height of the Starfish mutiny. Again I lived the moment of my degradation. Then just as suddenly I was spared the sight of it all" (*SS*, p. 37). These phallic figures ("Naked. Still wearing their steel helmets"), emerging where fear meets jealousy, are projections of Skipper's feelings of impotence, for they succeed with Cassandra where Skipper has failed: " 'Give me your gun, please' hanging her head, whispering, finger tracing meditative circles through the hair on his chest, 'please show me how to work your gun . . . ' " (*SS*, p. 43). Their existence seems to be a function of Skipper's struggling psyche, which represses them just after Cassandra's request for the leader's gun—"But he was gone. All three were gone." Skipper's jealous fear is also a key to the fact that immediately after the trio disappear, the bus emerges intact from "the dead center of some nightmare accident" (*SS*, p. 36); Skipper makes reference to Fernandez, Cassandra's husband and Skipper's rival.

Jealousy born of sexual frustration and a fear associated in his psyche with the resulting sense of impotence, a fear ultimately of homosexuality, is behind

34

the attack by Tremlow (the man in skirts). Skipper's rivalry with Fernandez (the homosexual whose name is tattooed on Skipper's chest), and, in part, Skipper's efforts to protect his daughter from Jomo (the one-armed man on the first island). Skipper wants from Cassandra the fidelity that his alter ego, Sonny, the "mess-boy" on the ship Skipper captained, insists upon: "Damn all those unfaithful lovers" (*SS*, p. 24). Thus the toast Skipper asks Cassandra to join him in (she doesn't) is the same toast he asks Fernandez to drink while driving to the motel after their wedding: "But a toast, Fernandez, to love and fidelity, eh Cassandra?" (*SS*, p. 117). One of the basic problems that Skipper must overcome is that the Hencher-like comfort Skipper needs (as reflected in his repeated references to "safe" and "secure") can be fulfilled only by woman as mother—Cassandra treats her father like a child and he seems to like it. Though there is something deathly about the idea of Family, as seen in the suicide of Skipper's father and the subsequent disappearance of his mother, perhaps *because* his family destroyed itself, Skipper longs for the Order that the Navy provides—"Shore Patrol, and so protected, protecting" (*SS*, p. 10).

As is the case in *The Beetle Leg* and *The Lime Twig*, Hawkes's characters interlock psychologically. The most obvious example is Captain Red's connection with Skipper—both are captains, and though Captain Red does what Skipper at the stage of his encounter with Tremlow cannot do, control his ship, Red is described as "wind-whipped, tall and raw and bald like me" (*SS*, p. 70). Similarly, the key to Skipper's relationship with Miranda can be found in Miranda's relationship with Cassandra. Cassandra wears the green dress Miranda made for her, and Miranda seems to sense that this green dress will touch touch Skipper's nerve at Innocence and Desire. The connection between Miranda (who is dressed in black) and the sexuality suggested by Cassandra's dress is death: "Between the two of them always the black umbilicus" (Ibid.). Skipper's closeness to Sonny makes him more than a messboy; rather, the man who is said to have "invented" Skipper's name is the mate of Skipper's consciousness, very much part of what Skipper sees as himself: " 'Sonny,' looking around for him in the mirror, 'can't you give me a little help . . . ' " (*SS*, p. 130). Both Skipper and Sonny envision gentle islands, but it is Sonny's island (all its inhabitants are black)—"And I got a gentle island, too, if I can just find her. Wanders around some . . . " (*SS*, p. 24)—that is the truly gentle island Skipper finally reaches.

The islands in *Second Skin* are typical Hawkesian structures, paired, paradoxical, and causing the protagonist pain in getting there. The relationship between Skipper's self and the islands can be found in Melville's metaphor from *Moby Dick*: "In the soul of man lives one insular Tahiti, full of peace and joy, but encompassed by all the horrors of the half-known life." Skipper dreams of an island paradise, but he deceives himself by thinking he has reached his "gentle island" when in fact it is a cold Puritan existence that remains a horror until his "half-known life" becomes known. The polarity of the two islands, Caribbean and Atlantic, involves Skipper in overcoming a conflict that is the difference between life and the death associated with Miranda, and the rigid repetitive moral order of the islanders' existence: "Family and friends, then, gathering week after dreary week for the Sabbath, meeting together on the dangerous day of the Lord, pursuing our black entanglement, waiting around for something—first snow? first love? first outbreak of violence?" (*SS*, p. 55).

The fact that the narrator comes to recognize Miranda as nothing but a "Classical postcard from an old museum," realizing that she represents "Desire and disaster" (*SS*, p. 96), offers proof that Hawkes's narrator, unlike those which preceded him, has become capable of a degree of perception that makes possible Skipper's movement to the second, freer island—"kicked myself free of her, kicked my way out of the car and fled. Burning. Blinded. But applauding myself for the escape." But before Hawkes lands Skipper on the second island, Hawkes makes his self-avowed "victim" undergo a voyage as demanding and revealing of the individual as Jason's.

The greatest challenge Skipper must face is Tremlow, and the memory of Tremlow. Just prior to the "brutal act," Skipper makes the metaphorical connection between problems of the self and navigation: "I felt what it was like to be faintly smothered in some new problem of seamanship" (*SS*, p. 136). The ship's mutiny, the threat to Skipper's moral and military Order, seems inevitable, necessary, for Skipper does little to avert it, suppressing Sonny's warnings. There can be no doubt that the force Tremlow represents exists inside Skipper, and that this presence, like memory, surfaces and is repressed. Just before Skipper bumps with Uncle Billy, "who wore no underwear on bumping days" (*SS*, p. 90), Skipper is set upon by unseen forces which pelt him with snowballs (white the color of purity): and the pain of the second blow, not coincidentally corresponding to the second level of consciousness (the subconscious), reminds Skipper of Tremlow—"Tremlow, I thought, when the hard-packed snowball of the second hit burst into my face . . . " (*SS*, p. 87). Skipper, blinded by the snow, wants to fight this fear—"Tremlow! Come out and fight!"—but the fear remains unembodied, its manifestation as Tremlow existing entirely in Skipper's mind—"but I could find no enemy . . . Tremlow, if he had been there, was gone" (*SS*, p. 88). At this point Skipper makes the connection between Tremlow and Jomo, rival for his daughter at the dance—"I forgot about the demon of my past and began to muse about the enemy of the present who was, I knew, only too real." The connection between Skipper and his two adversaries is sexual; Skipper's morality and doubts about his potency, the keys to his fearful jealousy of Jomo, are thus linked to the threat of potential homosexuality from Tremlow. On the ship Tremlow's physical attack—"the grass skirt—wet rough matting of cruel grass—was rammed against me"—hits a moral nerve, " 'What the hell!' . . . And then: 'Dear God,' I said . . . " (*SS*, p. 47). But in terms of Skipper's survival and emergence on Catalina Kate's island, Tremlow's attack is successful, necessary like Cassandra's death; for although Skipper clings in the short term to the hope of religion—"It was Mac, Mac with his vestments flying and his tiny face white with fear, Mac who flung down the rope" (*SS*, p. 47)—Skipper's Order (naval and moral) has been effectively and positively shaken. Rather than capturing Tremlow and suppressing the mutiny, Skipper lets the mutineers escape in the life boats, and, in a subtle counterpoint to Skipper's setting aside "my torn grey copy of the serviceman's abridged edition of the New Testament" (*SS*, p. 136), says to Mac of Tremlow, " 'Let him go on dancing' " (*SS*, p. 148). This is an indication that Skipper's fear of Tremlow, which is finally a fear of himself, has been overcome in the confrontation. This change of direction in Skipper's self puts the second island within reach, as suggested midway through the scene by Skipper's metaphorical exchange with Sonny: " . . . he repeated the word: 'Turning.' 'Changing course, Sonny? Are we? Out with it, is she changing course to starboard?' 'Turning,' he repeated, 'turning to port' " (*SS*, p. 144).

The ship of Skipper's self is effectively turned, but the question of narrative perspective as the key to survival is raised one more time by the scene preceding Skipper's emergence with Catalina Kate, the scene in which Skipper for the last time is duped by appearances. Miranda's ruse, the decoy of Bub's hot-rod, succeeds, and Skipper arrives too late at the lighthouse to save Cassandra. When Skipper first encountered Miranda, the vision was puritanical, and the lighthouse was referred to as a "forbidden white tower." But if Skipper is to survive, it is clear that he must get to the source of that vision in order to overcome it: "that I could not escape the lighthouse, could do nothing to prevent my having at last to enter that wind-whistling place and having to feel my way to the top-most rung of its abandoned stair" (*SS*, p. 58).

Thus, though in one sense Skipper can blame Miranda for Cassandra's death—"She must have known since she arranged for the destruction, nursed it, brought it about, tormented both herself and myself with its imminence" (*SS*, p. 190)—as suggested earlier, Skipper also has himself to blame. Left on the beach by Bub and Miranda, Skipper is in Banks's position, "running after my destiny which always seemed to be racing ahead of me" (*SS*, p. 191). The orange, white and blue car with which Skipper chases after Bub's black beach buggy (with Miranda inside) is nicely described as a horse, "the aerial in whip position" (*SS*, p. 193).

Skipper's race with his destiny does not end (as Banks's does) with death, largely because he comes to terms with the inner conflicts that Banks could never put into perspective. Though the lighthouse frightens Skipper, it is essential to his survival that Skipper become one with the lighthouse: "I reached the bottom after all, and I sat on a concrete block in the empty doorway with my head in my hands. I sat there with my lighthouse on my shoulders" (*SS*, p. 199).

Skipper's triumph represents the attainment of the Tahiti that Melville suggested dwells in every man; Skipper, prefiguring Cyril's position in *The Blood Oranges*, goes so far as to say: "behind every frozen episode of that other island—and I am convinced that in its way it too was enchanted— . . . there lies the golden wheel of my hot sun" (*SS*, p. 48). Just as Skipper has changed ("the old smashed petty officer's cap"), so must Sunny, his psychic partner, who is described as "metamorphosed" (*SS*, p. 163).

And yet, the evidence beyond Hawkes's implicit judgment is that although Skipper has changed in the sense that he is now at peace with his present-tense reality, his values have changed very little. Though content that his island wanders, no longer the rock of morality that the Gentle Island represented, Skipper becomes not only master of his fate, but the authority figure present in his frustrated sense of order: "the leader now, and they were faithful followers, my entourage." Furthermore, Skipper's notion of love is still based on Innocence, a theme Hawkes returns to in the trilogy. Skipper says Catalina Kate "was like a child, like a young girl" (*SS*, p. 167), a clinging to the Image of Purity which will become so dangerous for the photographer, Hugh. That the love existing on Catalina Kate's island is positive is supported quite simply by the fact that it is working. And yet it is based on many of the suppositions that had once tortured Skipper. While "the green tattooed on my breast has all but disappeared" (*SS*, p. 47), what replaces it? There is still absolute Fidelity on the island, just as Sonny had dreamed, and this fidelity is based on an unnatural isolation from the outside world—Skipper and Sonny are the only male inhabitants on the island. A hint that Hawkes sees the dangers implicit here is contained in the ironic context in which the new family is set: "The mere lowing of a herd, you see, has become my triumph" (*SS*, p. 47), and in Hawkes's suggestion in an interview that the island contains "barbs . . . hidden beneath the flowers."

Thus, though Skipper has overcome certain problems of the self, and in so doing gone past the oppression which sealed *The Beetle Leg* between the first person voices of the Sheriff and Cap Leech, he has not either as a man or narrator reached the full potential suggested by the image of the lighthouse on his shoulders. The ultimate perspective and distance once again belongs to Hawkes, the ultimate controller of the binoculars in *The Lime Twig*. Skipper's escape from Miranda's island suggests Ulysses's triumph over Circe, but the way in which the chapters of Skipper's present-tense idyll alternate with sections representing the painful past suggests that Hawkes remains captivated by the basic rhythm of paradox that will be the cornerstone of the conflict sustaining his plays and trilogy.

WORDS ON ROCK BY PLEBIAN
THE LIME TWIG (1961)

"If the true purpose of the novel is to assume a significant shape and to objectify the terrifying similarity between the unconscious desires of the solitary man and the disruptive needs of the visible world, then the satiric writer, running maliciously at the head of the mob and creating the shape of his meaningful psychic paradox as he goes, will serve best the novel's purpose."

(John Hawkes, *Notes On The Wild Goose Chase*)

The Lime Twig belongs to a select handful of American novels—*The Scarlet Letter, Moby Dick, As I Lay Dying*—whose originality of vision is reflected in a form that cannot be classified as part of any specific genre. The term *romance novel* is not entirely appropriate here, because, though romance and novel are integrated with a degree of harmony that is in paradoxical relationship to the conflict within, the effect of the combination of romance with the varied use of novelistic narrative techniques is an intensity of vision that involves the reader in a wholly unique hybrid.

Published in 1961, *The Lime Twig* represents not only a synthesis of romance and novel, but a crossroads for a new generation of American fiction. Inadvertently signalling much of what has followed in the sixties and seventies, both thematically and structurally, *The Lime Twig*, like Barth's *Sot Weed Factor* and *Chimera*, Gardener's *Grendel,* and Barthelme's *The Dead Father*, looks both backwards and forward in time as a means of expressing the paradoxes and conflicts of the post-modernist world. The novel reflects theme (personal salvation through redemption) and form (the weave of romance images and metaphors) reminiscent of Hawthorne's nineteenth-century romance novels; but in its equally consistent and sophisticated understanding of the formal and thematic implications of multi-levelled narration, it also engages the reader in a unique way. The shifts in narration represent a dislocation of the reader's traditional distance, something as threatening to a reader's conception of reality as security as is Robbe-Grillet's *The Erasers*, another novel whose detective action leaves the reader with questions rather than answers. In this sense Hawkes parodies the genre, just as he parodies the western in *The Beetle Leg.*

In *The Lime Twig* the structure that houses the psyche central to the drama—Banks's—is the metaphor for the multi-levelled action. The unconnected single rooms in Lily Eastchip's wartime boarding house have been transformed under

38

the Banks management into three apartments containing four rooms each. One flat is rented to Hencher, one belongs to Michael and Margaret Banks (with Margaret's cat and Michael's horse), and the third, though apparently unoccupied is inhabited in Hencher's childhood memories by the Captain and Corporal who have become Larry and Sparrow in Banks's present-day mind. The number of rooms correspond to the number of men associated with the horse (or "housed") in Banks's mind: Hencher, who gives Banks the photograph, the image, and idea of the horse; Cowles, the horse's trainer; Jimmy Needles, Rock Castle's jockey; and Larry (with his appendage Sparrow), the boss, if not the horse's titular owner. As Hencher says: "But one of his four rooms is mine, surely mine" (*LT*, p. 24); and Hencher is right, his room is still intact, for to a great extent these figures (still far from realistic characters) exist, as Banks's two-storied house suggests, both at the level of Banks's consciousness and as part of his subconscious.

The three flats signal the importance of the number three in tightening and dramatizing the themes of the novel. The form of the novel speaks to an acceptance of the Renaissance notion that space is three-dimensional; and yet, though there are three separate levels of narration—Hencher's first person preamble, Slyter's prognostications, and the problematic third person omniscient narration—one hesitates to talk of separate points of view in Gide's terms. Both writers are interested in a shifting of distance; Hawkes tries to depersonalize the act of Perception. In suggesting that life is a question of perspective, Hawkes uses a pair of binoculars as the symbol and metaphor for this essential question of distance. In Hawkes's fiction, the artist is trying to put the self into perspective. Banks's rampant desire (symbolized by Rock Castle), now released after being so long repressed, destroys his ability to distinguish between the planes of dream and reality by leaving him in the limbo of a rhythm that alternates guilt and desire, the need for comfort with a need for sexual freedom. It is thus fitting that the binoculars should be first associated with the object of Banks' desire, Sybilline: "A giant pair of binoculars lay between her glass and his and the long strap was bound safely round her wrist" (*LT*, p. 98). These glasses are used to follow Rock Castle, and it is in this sense that the reader must contemplate the horse almost as an exercise in cubist perception; for as a symbol which moves into metaphor by gradations of meaning (the overlapping of related color and imagery), Rock Castle reverberates throughout *The Lime Twig* like a cubist guitar (a model of which Hawkes uses to good effect in *Second Skin*).

The primary power of Rock Castle as the novel's unifying metaphor is the way the lives of the characters and the imagery that accompanies them revolves around the central action: the discovery of the horse, and the preparation inside Banks for the final run. There are as many possible interpretations of what Rock Castle "is" as there are diverse reactions to the gold coin Ahab nailed to the mast of the *Pequod*. From photographic image to "live" animal, Rock Castle's emergence suggests the process by which the subconscious comes to the surface as consciousness. The scene which prefigures the process by which the bus rises to the surface of the canal in *The Blood Oranges*—"behind them the barge was sinking" (*LT*, p. 53)—is built on psychological metaphor—what exists on the Artemis already exists in Banks' mind: "once again—the Artemis was rolling—once again he saw the silver jaw, the enormous sheet, the upright body of the horse that was crashing in the floor of the Dreary Station flat" (*LT*, p. 39). As symbol and metaphor for Banks's subconscious, Rock

Castle represents both a heavy load and a force that goes off like a time bomb, as suggested by the difficulty in lifting the horse out of the hold of the *Artemis*: "Hencher was whispering, 'Ever see them lift the bombs out of craters?' " (*LT*, p. 51). The sense of past as present makes the image of the horse as timeless as memory itself: "He's ancient, Rock Castle is, an ancient horse and he's bloody well run beyond memory itself . . . " (*LT*, p. 39). As an image capable of change and movement, raised like Hester's "A" from the unconscious to the subconscious, from a vague personal awareness to an image which appears limitless and indefinable in public consciousness, the horse represents the form given to the artist's contemplation of the infinite. This is a synthesis at the level of the subconscious, not just of the unconscious and conscious, but of subjective and objective. It is in this sense that *The Lime Twig*, as signalled by Rock Castle's lineage, is not simply a parody of a psychological thriller, but is in itself a metaphor for artistic creation. Hawkes himself says in the "Insights" symposium: " 'Draftsman by Emperor's Hand . . . It all has to do with writing . . . 'Castle Churl by Draftsman out of Likely Castle by Cold Masonry' . . . drafting, building, both have to do with creating, writing, this low life, low life in a high kingdom. 'Castle Churl out of Words on Rock'—I think it's the 'Words on Rock' that are really important. The 'Words on Rock' are the book" (Insights, p. 84).

While Banks is Rock Castle's titular owner (he pays for it in the end), Larry owns the binoculars, which suggests that control of the horse and the ultimate focus of the many levels of the narrative structure is a problem of Perception. The pair of binoculars, first seen lying "between her glass and his," is an optical instrument operating inside the individual's mind like the actual object, necessary to focus on the grey space emerging out of the conflict of Comfort and Desire that repeatedly separates Hawkes's couples.

Banks does not pay much more attention to the binoculars than Sybil does, but there are indications that he should. Banks's problems with perception are signalled by the fact that he is an amateur horse player, a prognosticator afraid to back his instincts: "I've been picking them correctly. But not for cash . . . " (*LT*, p. 105). Banks's lack of perception, his eventual nose-to-nose immediacy with the horse, is the key to his failure to understand the emotional forces inside him, forces which lose the horse in frustration, separate him from Margaret, and make his reality an extension of Hencher's dream. Ironically, his emergence as a man of passion signals his failure as an artist figure: his control of the glasses is abandoned when his sexuality is aroused by the dance: "When they stood up, binoculars falling now against his hip . . . " (*LT*, p. 101). The paradox is unresolved in *The Lime Twig*: in order to enjoy himself, or in a sense become himself, Banks must overcome his guilt—"Only her own eyes were left and Banks could not frown at them. 'I'm a married man,' he said" (*LT*, p. 100)—and unharness his repressed sexuality; and yet, in trying to do so, he loses all perspective, all control of the situation: "But Banks didn't care. He heard the voice of the man and girl—they were ringed round him and the bodies curtained out all except a far-off anonymous noise from the crowd" (*LT*, p. 101). The intensity of Banks's sexual desires makes his reality an ongoing dream long after the binoculars have been returned to their owner, Larry. In the Baths, Banks struggles futilely to put the drama into focus, but in steam there is neither distance nor visibility, only the reality of the dream: "And the steam lay on the body of Jimmy Needles, and Cowles looked dead away. He thought he saw shadows through the puffs and billowing of the whiteness, and he longed more than anything for a towel, a scrap of cloth to clutch himself, to wipe against his eyes'' (*LT*, p. 114).

Banks's inability to perceive his situation makes his race a blind dream, and it is such lack of perspective that links Banks with Hencher, whose perception of minute detail represents a terrifying immediacy that makes Hencher a prisoner of his past, just as Banks becomes a prisoner of his present. It is in this sense that the Hencher/Banks problem is the reader's problem. The reader may also lose perspective, for, confronted with shifting levels of narration and the sheer intensity of the language, a reader may be radically disoriented.

Like Banks, threatened by an immersion in a sordid reality that offers no distance, no respite from a process which immerses him in truths about himself that he cannot recognize, the reader is instinctively drawn to the narrative voice of Sydney Slyter, whose surface wit represents humour as defence, distance as comfort. Slyter is "Your Sydney Slyter" (*LT*, p. 79) because his narration, the comfort of the surface rather than the threat of the subconscious, offers the illusion of confidence: "my prognosticians are always right" (*LT*, p. 80). This confidence is based on rational investigation. Slyter, a parody of the novelist, is an authority figure who, like the Sheriff in *The Beetle Leg*, seeks definitive answers through investigation; but just as the mining authorities mislead when they promise the dam will hold, Slyter's promises offer the reader the false hope of rational victory in a world whose forces defy rationality.

Perhaps what is most reassuring about Slyter's column is that it anchors the reader solidly in the present. Signalling what is essentially a novelistic rather than romance technique, Hawkes uses the tenses to great effect. The ongoing tension is between Time Past and Present. The description of the journey with the horse of the subconscious—"straight ahead lay darkness that was water" (*LT*, p. 54)—is suitably narrated in the past because of the basic connection between the subconscious process and memory. With the break to Banks at home, the narration shifts to the present tense—"The flat door is open and the cat sleeps." However, the reassurance of Present as surface reality is deceptive, for although Banks is physically at Home—" 'It's all right, Mrs Stickley,' she whispered, 'he's home now' " (*LT*, p. 56)—and absent from the scene of Hencher's death, Hencher is being kicked to death by the crazed horse of Banks's mind, a scene which undercuts the safety of Slyter's present as well, for the death of the man who lived in the part of the house that one could mark "Past" is described entirely in the present tense.

The metaphorical connection between Banks and Hencher is the House, Hawkes's frequent symbol of Comfort. Hencher has been so bombarded by life that he never wants to leave the protective confines; Banks tries to break out of the house, instinctively realizing with the frustration of the horse kicking in his parlor that he must release himself; and yet the further away he gets from Margaret and the Dreary Station flat, the more powerful is the alternating rhythm of guilt and comfort that draws him back.

As part of the household of Banks's mind, Hencher is in every sense "lodged." The irony is that Hencher should find what eludes Banks, a satisfaction with Order, an order suggested by the intact room that contains so much of his past (the red carpet, the screen behind which his mother changed, the "comforter," the memory of Reggie's Rose, a symbol of the two wars [the war over Europe and the war within]). Whether the fallen plane actually fits into the courtyard, or whether it just fell from the sky of this overgrown child's imagination, the dead pilot of Reggie's Rose exists in Hencher's mind as loss, and Loss is Vulcan in the underground mountain of the subconscious. A more immediate authority is necessary. Out of Hencher's painful psychic need for Comfort, Hencher, the child in the body of a fat man, "creates" living substitutes, "Michael and his wife," to whom as a lodger, a son of the roof, he can go for acceptance. Margaret accepts Hencher as he would want to be accepted—"His wife, Margaret, says I was a devoted son" (*LT*, p. 9)—Michael, however, takes offence when Hencher talks with or mentions Margaret; for, like Henry in *Charivari*, each male wants the mother figure to himself, not so much because he loves her as a woman, but because he fears losing her as a symbol of Comfort. Banks as a father surrogate is a projection of Hencher's needs, just as Hencher is a projection of Banks's guilt and fear: Hencher will die by the hooves of Banks's horse, but the death is as momentary as it is symbolic, despite the detectives' discovery of his corpse. What Hencher stands for—the Comfort associated with mother-love—lives on in Banks's subconscious.

The connection between Banks and Hencher is elaborately woven. On the *Artemis*, the ship named after the Goddess of Childbirth that transports Rock Castle, Banks is described as having "the eyes of a boy" (*LT*, p. 26). Just after Hencher brings up the "ownership" of Rock Castle, they see "a boy with the face of a man" (*LT*, p. 39), an apt description of both of them. As Hencher then tells Banks, "Ah, like me you are" (*LT*, p. 40). Banks, the child, is linked not ony to Hencher, but to Lovely, the stable boy, and Jimmy Needles, the jockey (a boy in size), who are squeezed in with them in the cab of the van which transports the Horse away from the water of the unconscious. Later, in the Baths, Banks is reduced to a child—"He felt how naked he was, how helpless. Then, still on all fours, he came to the corner" (*LT*, p. 116).

As the shift in narration at the beginning of the numbered chapters suggests, increasingly there seems to be evidence that Mr. Banks, the landlord, and William Hencher, the lodger, are unequal parts of a self that has difficulty distinguishing between the pronouns "I", "you", and "he." At different times the self is all three. Although the tone and style of the unnumbered chapter narrated by Hencher continues, we never again hear Hencher's first person voice. Having found temporary contentment with Margaret, his imaginary mother, the "I" disappears, becoming a "third person" like Banks, as if this same voice were now perceiving himself objectively as "Hencher" rather than subjectively as "I," as if someone else were now holding him at arm's length and examining him.

The complexity of the narration is reflected in Hawkes's handling of Time. In spite of Albert Guerard's prediction that Hawkes would move towards novelistic realism, the sense of time which governs *The Lime Twig* (and all of Hawkes's novels) is still essentially the indefinite time of Romance: "not Wednesday at all, only a time slipped off its cycle with hours and darkness never to be accounted for" (*LT*, p. 49). Time, like Hawkes's understanding of "reality" as a paradoxical mixture of subconscious and conscious forces, cannot for Hawkes effectively be depicted by the clearly definable temporal sequences of the Novel, but rather by the contemporaneous blend of past, present, and future suggested by "It was Tuesday next," the vertical sense of time one encounters in the romance novels of Hawthorne and in the novels of Joyce and Proust. Set within a conflict of horizontal time (Slyter's novelistic narrative) and vertical time (the Romance assumption), the key to the romance weave within the novelistic superstructure of *The Lime Twig* is a sentence prefiguring

Cyril's tapestry of love in *The Blood Oranges*: "In the dusk surrounding the Baths the bees swarmed straight off the klaxon and made a golden thread from the bicycle to a nearby shrouded tree" (*LT*, p. 118).

This line, concluding the description of Cowles's death in the Baths, is the key to the imagery of *The Lime Twig*. Next to the repetition of the image of Rock Castle—"the stallion's cyclic emergence again and again" (*LT*, p. 139)—the central image of this book is the lime. Traditionally, lime twigs were used to trap birds. The association of birds with Michael and Margaret, foreshadowing fresh moments of suffering, suggests that the Banks pair themselves are the trapped birds. Banks is a captive of his desire, Margaret remains a prisoner of "the roost".

If one presses the metaphor, as Hawkes does, further connections arise. A lime is a fruit of considerable surface beauty and inner bitterness, and the nature of this paradox is the key to much of Hawkes's imagery in *The Lime Twig*. Linked with the color green—Monica's "bright green dress" and Rock Castle's racing colors of green and black—the image recalls the painfully threatening sexuality of the "adventuress in green" in *Charivari*, and the close connection between sexuality, marriage and confinement in *The Cannibal*. The association with lime green makes the Horse an image of irresolvable paradox, both at the outset—"Michael himself . . . was tasting lime: smells of the men . . . smells of the horse" (*LT*, p. 54)—and just before the race—"the horse's mouth was filled with green scum." Perhaps most important in terms of the growth of the image into metaphor, lime green reflects the sense of time-lessness, the dream brought rushing back to reality, implied by the collision of man and horse, present and past, on the race track: "The green, the suspended time was gone" (*LT*, p. 170). The lime is not a static image, but one that suggests through repetition and weaving the interdependency of character and Time.

The lime emerges as the central image of paradox which, unresolved, results first in pain, then in death. Just as the scream of Cowles's death might have been the pleasurable scream of one of the bathers doused with cold water, the scene in the Baths where the lime sensation is reencountered is itself a sensuous hell, horrifying yet somehow appealing. The lime is Hawkes's ultimate metaphor for paradox, for, like the morphine with which Larry imprisons Sparrow, it promises beauty (relief) which is at best illusory since it contains and even heightens in its alternating rhythm a certain bitterness (pain).

The imagistic counterpoint to the lime image within the elaborate romance weave is the image of the pearl. Monica, who is Margaret's child counterpart (as Hencher was Michael's), wears her mother Sybilline's pearl hairpins in innocence; but the connection between the novel's female characters is first signalled when Banks, who is thinking of leaving the house, his head filled with "thoughts of night and pleasure he was about to find," finds one of Margaret's hairpins in his pocket. Margaret's hairpin, as opposed to Sybilline's, is not pearl-tipped—between Margaret and Michael there is only the painful pin. The sexual nature of the image becomes explicit, however, when Banks is with Sybilline: "She had given a single promise and three times already made it good, so now he knew her habits, knew what to expect, the commotion she could cause in bed . . . each time she lost a pearl—and she had lost three pearls" (*LT*, p. 141).

Again the imagery brings one back to the question of perspective. Not only does Banks, lost in the present of his sexual fantasy, have difficulty in finding

Sybilline's hairpins, but, faced with "the hard tiny tear of pearl on its needle shank" (*LT*, p. 142), Banks sees only the pearl, failing to see the pain that Hawkes seems to suggest is at the end of such sexuality. Thus, Banks's problem is not unlike Hugh's in *The Blood Oranges*, for he tends to be attracted by what he mistakenly sees as the pure and innocent in beauty, the Virgin. The language of the following sentence suggests a repression of the very sexuality that might otherwise have been enjoyed: "her fresh poses making his own dead self fire *as if he had never touched her* and making her body look tight and *childish* as if *she had never been possessed by him*" (*LT*, p. 142). Like Margaret's beating by Thick and rape by Larry, Michael's acting out of his sexual needs and fantasies with Sybil represents an eroticism based in fear, not joy. Sybilline is the Sybil in the epigraph of Eliot's *The Wasteland*—to desire Sibyl is to desire death. Banks finds sexual outlet, but ultimately it is destructive, for sex represents temptation for Banks. He learns about Sybilline in the Men's room, and his initial shame ("He tried to look away, but the man went on with his whispering, 'I've got a word for you: *Sybilline's in the Pavilion*. Do you understand? *Sybilline's in the Pavilion* . . . ' " [*LT*, p. 93]) is the source of his later arousal. Initially Banks's desire is repressed, and his essential puritanism—the relegation of wife to Home, and sexuality to drunken male fantasy—is as deep in his psyche as Rock Castle.

The importance of the pearl and lime imagery in the vast web of *The Lime Twig*'s inner romance weave is their essentially paradoxical nature. There is pain at the end of beauty (the pearl hairpin) and bitterness inside the surface beauty of the lime; and the dramatization of such paradox is most clearly seen in the master/slave relationship between Larry and Sparrow. The needle which Larry uses to put Sparrow momentarily into the calm of dream reality suggests also the pain and desperate emptiness and loss that both Hencher and Banks feel, the emptiness that follows as soon as the pearl of relief wears off. Based on the pearl/lime metaphors, the Larry/Sparrow relationship is of further importance because it signals Hawkes's use of counterpoint with characters as well as images. At the ultimate dualistic level of dream reality—the focus through which the reader perceives things—image and character are on equal footing: what in the past tense of Hencher's mind was the Captain and the Corporal (who relies on the Captain's needle for his wounds), inhabit Banks's present tense reality as Larry and Sparrow.

One can see the way Hawkes creates this romance sense of character as image in the progression of deaths whose interlockings are the only structure to Banks's galloping psyche. The Banks/Hencher connection is reprised in the Hencher/Cowles relationship. Such paired, psychologically interlocking relationships, first seen in *The Beetle Leg*, are signalled either by physical positioning (Hencher and Banks sitting opposite and then parallel to each other on the *Artemis*; Banks with Cowles in the steam [" 'Lie next to me, Mr Banks,' and Cowles helped him up . . . "] [*LT*, p. 153]); by double entendre, particularly in pronoun usage such as "he himself," or by the use of doors. The door of the Banks flat is open, Comfort on one side and Sexuality on the other; there are double doors on Rock Castle's paddock, suggesting the paradox of the horse metaphor; and Larry's limousine is described as having double doors. The refinement of the pairs in *The Lime Twig* over the Sheriff/Wade or Bohn/Finn associations in *The Beetle Leg* is significant; in the later novel, one can watch the characters grow into each other like images in a dream. The Hencher/Cowles relationship does not represent the more static psychological relationship of the Sheriff and his deputy.

Physically, Cowles and Hencher are virtually doubles—"then Cowles is vomiting into the tall grass—he is a fat man and a man as fat as himself lies inside the van" (*LT*, p. 112)—but the connection is not just physical, for it seems likely that Cowles becomes sick not so much by the sight of Hencher's death as by a vision of his own. As Hencher is virtually suffocated by the Horse, Cowles, sharing Hencher's unspeakable horror, experiences his own death prematurely: "And Cowles shouts, doubles over then as powerless as Hencher in the van" (*LT*, p. 60). The connection between their deaths is made even more convincing by the fact that the description does not focus on Hencher dying, but on Cowles reacting.

One usually would not speak of characters in terms of counterpoint, yet this term, more appropriate to imagery or musical phrasing, applies as well to the figures which come in and out of focus in Banks's dream reality. Trapped underground in the Men's Room (psychologically in the subconscious), Banks is confronted by three men carrying Rock Castle placards and the picture of a nude woman—the suggestion of Rock Castle as the horse of Desire, the image of the nude woman foreshadowing their temptation of Banks with Sybilline. This system of three—"They were a system—'eunuchs', Cowles called them, 'the mathematicians' " (*LT*, p. 60)—is linked to the three figures (Larry, Sparrow, Thick) who murder Cowles at the Baths.

Hencher did not have a father, and felt the psychic need to create one, first out of the dead pilot of Reggie's Rose, and then out of Michael Banks; so also does Banks make an authority figure for himself out of the repression that exists inside himself. Larry clearly represents the repressive side of Banks's desire, and as such is a repressive weight for Banks: "The man was big, heavy as a horse cart of stone" (*LT*, p. 100). Though Banks finally breaks free from this authority figure who alternatingly titillates and represses his sexual drive, the same authoritarian control over Banks is exercised by Larry for the same reason he can make Sparrow his slave: Larry does not feel. Both a creation of Banks's unconscious and a small-time crook, Larry is invulnerable: "Larry . . . lifted a vest of linked steel . . . It fit over the undervest like silk" (*LT*, p. 73); and as the same sort of medicine man as Cap Leech—"The tip of the needle dribbled a bit. He had tended to Sparrow in alleys, bathhouses with crabs and starfish dead on the floors, in doorways in the Majesty, and the back of horsedrawn wagons on stormy nights" (*LT*, p. 80)—he sees only what he needs to in order to dominate. "He's God", Hawkes has said. Certainly when Larry, "who was an angel if any angel ever had eyes like his or flesh like his" (*LT*, p. 159), rapes Margaret to avenge Michael's night with Sybil, he acts as an angel of retribution.

Larry is the force that both separates and unites Margaret and Michael. The bond between husband and wife is fear. In *Beyond the Wasteland*, Raymond Olderman, recalling the fishing metaphor in *The Beetle Leg*, offers a useful interpretation: "Beaten and cut Margaret sees Larry dressed only in his bullet-proof vest and notes 'the shiny fish-like scale'. Larry is the fish brought to the surface by Margaret and Michael's desires, but instead of the simple fertility symbol sought by the wounded Fisher King, they have landed an inverted symbol of potential self-violence and death" (p. 160). Insight into this link between Margaret and Michael can be found in the counterpoint of Larry's relationship to Michael, Little Dora's domination of Margaret. Little Dora possesses much of Larry's authoritarian omniscience, and the similarity in their almost deific powers results because Little Dora (a wonderful name for a Dickens figure) shares Larry's uncanny power of perception. It is Dora who asks Larry if he saw "the item" in the paper, a reference to the Slyter interview that precipitates Cowles's murder. When she addresses Margaret as "Mrs Banks" while Maragaret is still wondering why this stranger has waved to her at Dreary Station, her powers seem beyond explanation, at least to Margaret. What is more, Little Dora shares her man Larry's instinct for what causes pain, though she inflicts it only psychologically. "What have you done with the kiddies?" (*LT*, p. 70), she asks Margaret almost immediately, thus triggering Margaret's horrible vision of children tied up and crushed under the train, and the painful admission, "Done with them? I've done nothing with them. There aren't any children" (*LT*, p. 71).

What finally differentiates Little Nora from Larry as a god is her domestic role: the woman repeatedly shows her weakness for man by asking Larry when he will drop by "the Roost." Similarly, Margaret's problem, recalling Lou's imprisonment and similar sexual fantasy in *The Beetle Leg*, and prefiguring Catherine's in *The Blood Oranges*, is that she is a domesticated animal who regards her husband as a God (Michael is always present as an Image in Margaret's mind). This servitude which defines woman as Wife is described very early in the book as a legal absolute: "She was Banks's wife by the law, she was Margaret . . . A wife would always ride through the night if bidden" (*LT*, p. 70). Although Little Dora shows signs of frustration with her role at Home, her fear of abandonment prevails: " 'Wait!' said Little Dora. 'You don't mean you're going without me, Larry! You wouldn't leave Little Dora behind! Not another day in the Roost . . . What the hell, I'm no matron . . . " (*LT*, p. 90). It is in this sense that the reality Hawkes's women face is less satisfactory than that of the men, for they do not exist for themselves, but rather as appendages to their men. However, though Margaret is described as "a girl with a band on her finger and poor handwriting, and there was no other world for her" (*LT*, p. 99), the emphasis should perhaps be put on the second phrase; by 1960 standards it is too early to call Hawkes a "womanizer" just because he shows the oppressiveness (often through prison-related imagery) that is woman's reality as he sees it.

Margaret's plight, for instance, parallels Michael's. Just as Banks's psyche is crowded by four men, there are four females who inhabit Margaret's mind (as well as her outer reality) in a fashion so subtle that she, like Banks, is largely unaware of the reason for her imprisonment and the reasons for her pain. In fact, her psychic defence of forgetting is so well developed—"Margaret remembered nothing"; "I don't remember much of when I was a child" (*LT*, p. 71)—that she is able to block out her torture, or experience it as pleasure.

And yet, typical of Hawkesian paradox, Margaret's struggle is also essentially different than Banks'. Though her beating by Thick/Larry links her to Banks in self-repression (in this sense her fantasy also makes Margaret her own prisoner), she is also prisoner of a heritage, the heritage of woman's fear of being alone: "Knowing how much she feared his dreams: knowing that her own worst dream was one day to find him gone" (*LT*, p. 33). "I'm dead to the world" (*LT*, p. 60), she says when Banks leaves the afternoon after Hencher's death; "Where will Michael be?" (*LT*, p. 76), she keeps asking when he is gone. Margaret's devotion to her role as wife causes her to lose her identity: "Thick had burned her things, identification card and all" (*LT*, p. 135); and she discovers painfully that as an image of Innocence ("a child anything could be done to"), she has no freedom: "decided to try just how much freedom she really had . . . Then he came at her with a truncheon" (*LT*, pp. 126-7). Margaret's abandonment is remarkably like Hester's in *The Scarlet Letter*: "And thus much of woman there was in Hester, that she could not scarcely forgive him . . . for being able to withdraw himself so completely from their mutual world, while she groped darkly and stretched forth her cold hands and found him not" (p. 125).

Finally, in terms of the convolutions of the novel, Margaret is Banks's prisoner, left in confinement above all because of his inability to come to terms with his Trojan horse, his inability to free himself and thus be able to return and free her (there is no evidence until Fiona in *The Blood Oranges* that women can control their own destinies or liberate themselves). It is not altogether surprising, however, that Banks cannot return to Margaret, for the imagery suggests that Margaret, now the mother figure, is part of the horse with which Banks is so obsessed. Margaret, a thoroughly domesticated beast who earlier is described as smelling of the "dust that gathers in the four rooms," is tethered to the bed in Dora's room; and after Thick and Larry apparently rope, break, and rape her, we read: "she now knew the hunger of the abducted . . . 4 a.m. and she was one of the abducted" (*LT*, p. 125). It is Rock Castle, the "prisoner of heritage in victorious form" (*LT*, p. 24), who is abducted from the stable. The connection suggests, however, that Margaret, a prisoner of heritage in defeated form (woman as wife), is not entirely abandoned, for, though abducted like the horse, she continues to ride in Banks's mind.

Margaret's "neighbor," Annie, represents both the innocence that Banks tries to preserve as Image, and a bridge between his subconscious (the deep morality that needs to believe in Innocence and Purity) and his consciousness, as suggested by his futile efforts to save this "child in a bright green dress" "Because he recognized the child—she had always been coming over a bridge for him . . . And he kept driving the man, fighting the constable farther and farther away from the dead child . . . " (*LT*, p. 161). Hawkes says of the scene: "He's alone at the time that Margaret is alone with Larry, and he's alone with a child being killed on the street which is possibly an analogue of Margaret . . . it's pretty clear that the spirit of Margaret—Margaret is a child—the spirit of her is being shot to death in proximity to Michael by, ironically, the police force, while Margaret herself is being really brought to death by Larry" (Insights, p. 95). It should also be noted that the gun whose shot represents the death of childhood innocence is also the shot that starts Banks's final race: "The shot went off just below his window . . . he thought of Jimmy Needles . . . Then he was out of bed, across the room and running . . . " (*LT*, p. 160). Though dead as an image of Innocence—the young girl in the green dress suggesting Margaret and Monica (Margaret was dressed in green before the beating, and after it, "Monica dressed herself in the discarded green dress" [*LT*, p. 135])—Annie reappears at the paddock as an outgrowth of Banks's jealousy. Despite Banks's effort to repress her presence—"you haven't any business here!"—Annie fulfills her fantasy, expressed to Margaret at the outset, by kissing the jockey, the man capable of riding the Horse. Though Annie is primarily a function of Banks's past, she exists in the present for Margaret, first in Margaret's psyche ("Something was coming toward the window and it made her lonely"), and then, reminiscent of Rock Castle's transformation from image to kicking beast, in physical form: "Annie had come to the adjoining window" (*LT*, p. 63). Though Margaret offers to bring Annie along when she goes to see Michael (a proposition he refuses), the way in which Annie appears and fades away suggests that she is Margaret's friend and neighbor primarily in the sense that loneliness and fear create company in images.

As pure an image as any character can be, Annie's mutability hints that she exists in the grey space that separates Margaret and Michael as something shared, the child of the physical union they never have. While Margaret and Michael's relationship to Annie further defines what this grey space is—inoperative notions of Innocence and Purity linked inextricably with Guilt, Fear, and Jealousy—Annie is finally as difficult to define as Pearl in *The Scarlet Letter*. Annie represents something that exists deep in the subconscious past (Hencher recalls that the bomber fell while he was listening "to the sounds of the wireless from Annie's window"), and she is the key that unlocks the last vault at the bottom of Banks's psyche. But Annie remains a mystery that Hawkes purposely leaves unresolved for readers who would find an answer to every problem.

The grey ground where Annie exists becomes the fog in which the detectives in the last chapter search for clues to Hencher's depth. The reader's hold on reality is shattered—as is the idea of Knowledge as the handle of the door which Hawkes leaves open between dream and reality—because detective work does not pay: Slyter does not pick the winner, the detectives have no answer to who killed Hencher; in fact, the reader who has done his detective work and discovered that Hencher exists partially in Banks's psyche may be surprised that there is a corpse at all.

The radical shifting in focus of the binoculars suggests that life is like Banks's race: "it ceases to be motion, but at its peak becomes the long downhill deathless gliding of a dream" (*LT*, p. 171). Banks finally ignores the binoculars; he lacks the necessary distancing apparatus for survival: "And he had the view that a photographer might have except that there was no camera, no truck's tailgate to stand upon" (*LT*, p. 170). Slyter has the distance necessary for survival, but his detective work is meaningless because he believes in an operative equation of winning and losing (in the end nobody wins the race). This fails to account for paradox, the combination of forces as seemingly polar as dream and reality. Similarly, Larry's power is finally meaningless, for Larry is blindly authoritarian and fails to see the potential role of Banks's self in the race: "He's crossed us, he's crossed us, hasn't he?" (*LT*, p. 171). His vision is distorted by the green lenses of his glasses, and Larry asks Sybil to return the binoculars—" 'Let me have the binoculars, Sybilline.' Larry removed his green glasses"—but it is too late. The reality that seemed to exist as a function of Larry's deific vision of the world takes an unexpected turn; Banks is already breaking loose from his repressive nature and becoming one with the horse of desire: "he began to trot, shoes landing softly, irregularly on the dirt" (*LT*, p. 170).

Banks's death is intended to represent his redemption—"And redeemed, he has been redeemed" (*LT*, p. 163); and this race to death and redemption, typical of the sense of helplessness Olderman sees as emblematic of protagonists in novels of the 1960s ("the protagonist's sense of helplessness even as he proceeds to the confrontation" [*BtW*, p. 61]), is a paradox. Banks's final effort to control his destiny is both a triumph and a failure, for although he may be redeemed, he is also dead; and, "despite the sacrifice and redemption of the individual, the wasteland itself continues, for memory and desire continue."

Banks dies like Hugh in *The Blood Oranges*, that is, like Christ in a crucifixion pose, "the arms out, the head thrown back"; his death signals a turning point in Hawkes's work: the individual has started to take responsibility for his self. It is the first evidence in Hawkes's work of the *possibility* of an individual mastering his fate; and as Banks is unable to do so and brings about his own destruction in the effort, the sporadic references to Hamlet are, in this context, appropriate. Certainly the theme of the irreversible fate is graciously borrowed in metaphor. Banks, like Hamlet, is felled by encountering too much in the dark recesses of his mind. Hawkes does not belabor the connection, nor does he overwork his other literary allusions. The Golden Bowl, the name of the race, is a competition on another level that Hawkes has with Henry James, author of that other masterpiece of form; Marlowe's "Pippet" is the frontrunner no one remembers when they have seen the Prince of Denmark's entry.

The question of fate and the individual's control over his self does, however, raise the final issue. Banks's death, like the multi-levelled narration that ends in mystery, takes the reader back to the question of omniscience signalled earlier by Slyter's statement, "Someone knew it all before." All evidence points to the fact that the ultimate owner of the binoculars, the man who masters the Horse by being able to bring it in and out of focus, is Hawkes himself. Having created a world where the line between dream and reality, subconscious and conscious states, has been erased, the creator emerges as the only figure with sufficient distance, with the proper balance between polar forces, to survive. While Hawkes likes to disassociate the writer from the creation—and certainly there is plenty to be said about the work of art without considering the artist—the role of the Artist in relationship to the Man, which becomes a central issue in the trilogy, is signalled in *The Lime Twig* not only by the shifts of narration and tense, by also by the sense that an omniscient presence is manipulating the fate of his characters like a God: "But there was better than this in wait for him, something much better" (*LT*, p. 36). Hawkes himself makes the connection between the human and artistic needs in Banks; saying in Interview that Banks "instinctively must have felt the human and artistic need to arrive at a resolution that would be somehow redemptive" (*John Hawkes on his Novels*, p. 457). If Banks's self represents both artistic and human needs, surely the writer who manipulates this self's fate is involved, if not personally in the sense that some writers dramatize their own lives, then certainly from what lies behind that point of view, Hawkes's moral and artistic outlook on life. Thus, *The Lime Twig*, representing the first instance of an individual taking responsbility for his self, marks an important turn in Hawkes's fiction, the partial breakaway from the authoritarian narrative structure of his earlier work. The link between artist and protagonist grows out of Skipper's voyage of the self in *Second Skin* into the trilogy.

THE ICEBERG SURFACES
THE BLOOD ORANGES (1971), *DEATH, SLEEP AND THE TRAVELER* (1973), *TRAVESTY* (1976)

"what may not be so obvious is that, as I mentioned today, I would have been a romantic poet if I had not lived now, and I think that what I have written in *The Blood Oranges* and *Death, Sleep and the Traveler* and in my last novel, is in fact a triad, not a trilogy, a triad of fictions which are in fact about sexuality and the romantic imagination in an absurdist world . . ."

(John Hawkes in *TREMA*, Paris III)

In Hawkes's work through *Second Skin*, one gets meaning from the maze of images and metaphors in direct proportion to the amount of time one spends digging beneath the surface in an effort to make the elusive connections between image and idea. In *The Blood Oranges*, and more strikingly in *Death, Sleep and the Traveler*, the process in terms of structural complexity and linguistic simplicity seems reversed. Ideas which once hid in metaphors of thickly-layered sentences are often revealed directly. Whereas in the early work Hawkes challenged the reader to use his imagination in a process of searching and reconstruction, in *The Blood Oranges* Hawkes offers the reader guidelines, words like "psyche," "the self," "consciousness," which help the uninitiated to grasp what appeared earlier only as motorcycles, red wagons, race horses, and limes. Much of Hawkes's language remains opposed to the realism of recorded detail, as when his narrator states: "Need I insist that the only enemy of the mature marriage is monogamy?" or "each of us was witness to the other three, I knew that individual and group consciousness was mounting." Authorial self-consciousness seems to have shifted the burden from the *suggestion* of image and metaphor, the romance way, to the more prosaic method of *telling* associated with the novel proper.

Much is made in the interview with Robert Scholes of the Illyric quality in *The Blood Oranges*. In the tie between "romance" and "love" Cyril's idyll comes closest to Orsino's Illyria: novel and play share an artist's interest in the workings of Love. Hawkes emphasizes here the role of the Imagination in combating constricting morality, his latent puritanism and America's: "Illyria doesn't exist unless you bring it into being" (Bellamy, *The New Fiction*, p. 106). This attitude of imaginative self-reliance is in contrast to Olivia's standard Christian acceptance of Fate:

> "*Fate show thy Force; ourselves we do not owe.*
> *What is decreed must be, and be this so*"
> (*I*, 5, 300-301);

and Cyril's "anything that lies in the palm of love is good" (*BO*, p. 58) is in keeping with Feste's belief—Feste suggesting Cyril as "love singer"—in the necessity of seizing love in the present:

> "*What is love? 'Tis not hereafter;*
> *Present mirth hath present laughter,*
> *What's to come is still unsure*"
> (*II*, 3, 45-48).

It is where sexuality and imagination connect in Hawkes—"these three fictions very consciously . . . have to do with the imagination and trying to use sexuality as a means of exploring the imagination or exposing it. Sexuality and imagination. These opposites always appear." (*TREMA*, Paris III, p. 263)—that the role of artist becomes essential to resolving the paradoxes of morality. In *The Blood Oranges*, sexuality and imagination are direct reflections of how Cyril and Hugh see the world; their outlook on life is seen in the varying degrees of their sexual freedom, which in turn is a metaphor for their imaginative/artistic capabilities. The central metaphorical struggle between Love and Death, Eros and Thanatos, arises out of the differences between Cyril and Hugh, differences that make one a "singer", the other a victim of Love. These differences reflecting the paradox that enables *The Blood Oranges* to be both a song of love and the death of the romantic artist.

The paradoxical give and take between the apparent polarity of Cyril (the artist as Man, the outer, healthier world suggested by his grape arbour and affinity for the sun), and Hugh (the artist in whom the man is dead, the dark room, images imprisoned in the inner world) is reflected not only in the opposition of colours—Cyril's is predominantly golden, Hugh's black like his inner night—but in the very form of the novel, a weave of time in which present precedes past and becomes the future.

Cyril, the most positively portrayed and hopeful character in Hawkes's fiction, is an artist of Love because he gives expression to his imaginative and passionate forces. Cyril's belief in free will, the necessity of creating one's own Illyria that Hawkes mentioned earlier, gives him the strength of a god over those around him; but his godhood is defined not as an omniscient, infallible religious Being, but in the positive sense of daemon, a spirit capable of waning, as it does when the weight of Hugh's "medieval side", his self-destructive romanticism, becomes oppressive.

Speaking to the power of his imagination and the freedom of his sexuality, Cyril, unlike Banks, Hugh, and the others, is free from guilt. Though Cyril will admit to twinges of pain natural in a "man of feeling," he will not willingly share Hugh's agony: "was this at least my true pain, my real agony . . . Not at all . . . externals of pain that belonged to Hugh but never to me" (*BO*, p. 57). By contrast, Hugh, the photographer as artist, is a failure in love and in art because his vision of the world, reflected in his morality and in his photography, is that of the self-destructive romantic.

Artist and romantic are one in the contemplation of Beauty. Both seek out images of beauty, and both become painfully aware that the pure image inevitably comes closer to an idea of perfection than any actual art work or woman. Indeed, part of what makes man and artist a romantic is the self-defeating corollary that paradise—pure Beauty or Love—is unattainable. Love for the romantic artist is frequently a desire for pure beauty that remains an unattainable image.

It is not coincidental that, contained in the figure of Hugh, the romantic artist is a puritan of the first order, the man Cyril has in mind when he says "For some love is a crime" (*BO*, p. 36). The figure of the virgin which obsesses Hugh and Hawkes is perhaps the ultimate in romantic masochism; having sex with her would mean to the puritanical mind the destruction of what makes the image pure, a rape of the unspoiled wilderness of the child. For Hugh, artist and man, the connection is clearly made between virgin and mother: "Most of the faces of these peasant nudes are just fat and happy. They're all mothers with or without children" (*BO*, p. 64). Thus, Hugh will not have sex with Rosella or his other subjects, because, to the extent that Hugh's contemplation of the models makes them virgin mothers, making love to them would arouse the guilt of incest. Fiona is largely untouched by Hugh; by assuming Catherine's role of mother, she brings out her innate quality of Mother (she calls all men "baby"). In Hugh, contemplation of the image by the artist denies physical pleasure to the man, a denial of Eros which in Hugh shows itself in possessiveness—"he persecuted himself and begrudged me Catherine" (*BO*, p. 58)—and jealousy—"the rage and fear that shrivels your ordinary man at the first hint of the multiplicity of love."

Self-denial, the strange but inevitable end to the romantic's self-indulgence, is the rope that links Hugh with Christ. Hawkes ties the ends together carefully—Hugh is first referred to as "St Peter in stone" (*BO*, p. 31), which becomes "my courageous self-betraying St Peter" (*BO*, p. 33), the "self-betrayal" a clue to the romantic's self-destructive nature. Most significantly, Hugh sees himself as a Christ figure: "(Hugh) who always said that his long thin legs were the legs of Christ" (*BO*, p. 211). It is his insistence on perfection, Love idealized to impossible proportions, that links Hugh with Christ, and is clearly at the heart of his problems as a photographer/artist: "There she is. See her? Perfect, perfect!" (*BO*, p. 58). It is Hawkes who suggests that the Christ connection is destructive, negative: "Kuehl: Although one finds no god in your fiction, many of your characters are identified with Christ—for example Ernst in *The Cannibal*. Hawkes: But that's a negative association isn't it? When Ernst is fanatically involved with the little carvings of Christ, he is approaching his own death in an absurd way" (Kuehl, p. 161).

As seen earlier in the dependence on Zizendorf as a symbol of the Father, and in Banks' and Camper's alternating rhythm of desire and the need for security associated with their wives, the ongoing conflict in Hawkes's work between Security and Passion first arises in *The Blood Oranges* with Cyril's seemingly paradoxical statement, "I am not opposed to domesticity." Although Cyril later displays some of the same needs for Security that are within Hugh, Cyril, the singer of sexual freedom, is not unsympathetic to the need for security; what he does oppose is the routine of domesticity, in which repetition dulls the senses and makes a job out of love-making. Cyril's statement is strategically placed, for it follows the section, the beginning that is the end, in which Cyril has fallen off the wall on which the "two enormous gamebirds" were "locked in love" (*BO*, p. 14), holding on almost as much as Catherine, who has sought sanctuary in a whitewashed retreat, to a living security blanket—"I too have begun to hold the larger of the two rabbits" (*BO*, p. 21). Significantly, "both of the rabbits are female," and it is the feeling of safety far from the dangers and joys of sexuality that causes Cyril to close with "An excellent basis for sexless matrimony . . . " This comment makes a strong transition to the next section's theme of domesticity, the need for Security in Cyril as a result of the apparent pain of sexuality, the first indication of the link between the apparent opposites that Cyril and Hugh represent.

But though Cyril will end clinging to security out of a sense of loss, rather than guilt over Hugh's death, his willingness to accept the complex, often diverse sexual needs of modern psyches comes from a point of view clearly at odds with conventional order: "It was I, after all, who was once more touching flame to the idea of the family and lighting anew the possibilities of sex in the domestic landscape" (*BO*, p. 89). What Cyril has in mind—though the success of his idyll would ultimately preserve the institution of marriage rather than destroy it—is a complete reversal of thinking, dramatized by Fiona and Cyril's efforts to exchange roles with Hugh and Catherine, so that the couple locked into marriage would be able to feel again passion and life: "I was waiting for the parents to become lovers and the lovers parents."

By contrast, Hugh's fear, symbolized by "the wedding ring worn bizarrely, ferociously" (*BO*, p. 92)—the circle of law in miniature skillfully reprised by Hugh's discovery of the circle of repression, the chastity belt—is first suggested by the male bird Cyril observes while sitting on the broken-down bicycle. This in turn speaks to the present state of his sexuality. The male of the species is above the smaller female, but in spite of this apparent position of dominance, the male seems threatened; at the very height of pleasure, it is the male who is in need of physical (and in Hawkes, physical action is inevitable metaphor for the psychological) defenses: "by flapping his wings and turning his entire shape into a great slowly hovering blue shield beneath which his sudden act of love was undeniable" (*BO*, p. 16). The "blue shield" suggests that the male has something to fear from the female in the very act which brings them closest together.

The final problem in this pain/love area comes from the fact that at one stage Cyril, Hawkes's mouthpiece, actually seems to celebrate, not simply recognize the possibility, of pain arising from the extended emotional state of love: "most of us enjoy the occasional sound of pain, though it approaches agony. In fact, could any perfect marriage exist without hostile silences, without shadows, without sour notes? Obviously not" (*BO*, p. 55). An alternating note of pain exists not only in the depiction of Hugh and Catherine's conventional marriage, but in Cyril's symbolic union with Catherine. Once again, Hawkes makes his point metaphorically rather than through dialogue and character interaction. The "marriage" between Cyril and Catherine is portrayed in terms of the white ship. The union begins with the separation of man and woman by symbols of Order and Family: "In one single instant priest and children and barefoot men, and white boat were poised above us. Suddenly Catherine and I were thrust on opposite sides of the narrow street" (*BO*, p. 122). The white boat is an apt symbol, for it suggests both the positive and negative aspects of marriage. As a symbol of purity, it is as destructive and overly idealistic as Hugh's ideas are—hence "the lunging, destructive descent of the white boat" (*BO*, p. 122)—but "the golden fish on the prow," linked with Cyril's gold, is what makes the union positive. The motion of the ship functions like the final question a minister poses at the marriage ceremony: "And if the enormous white sun-struck prow then veered toward Catherine, veered toward me?" The marriage is further invoked by white flowers: "high on the prow they had fastened a handful of Labularia maritima," flowers of the sea appropriate for the launching into water, symbol of consciousness that accounts for the pain in spite of the apparent security of the vessel. "The empty white boat was sliding painfully but safely" (*BO*, p. 126).

The alternative to the pain that continues in Catherine as the pull between Sexuality and Domestic Security is foreshadowed by the union of orange and white. The figure offered for contemplation is the pink statue of a human figure which has a black hole where its sexual parts would be. Although Hawkes avoids any suggestion of bisexuality as an alternative, Cyril's discovery implies that the willingness to accept paradox in sexuality is essential to survival. Fiona, the "faun" free of soceity's rigid definitions, tries to make Hugh see the figure as a hermaphrodite—"the beautiful stone figure was really a little boy as well as a little girl"—but Hugh is unable to see "the statue's double nature" (*BO*, p. 170) because his sense of inner order demands black or white.

Like his daughter, Meredith, Hugh cannot open himself to what is beautiful and free in nature; his state of mind is described as "those ancient tightly secured shutters." The dramatic representation of Hugh's self-imprisoning psyche is again conveyed in terms of romance technique, image and metaphor doing the work of character. The journey into the territory of paradoxical opposites—"peace and treachery, space and confinement"—represents a trip inside the fortress of Hugh's self. The entrance to the fortress is through the womb, the primal source of the life/pain paradox central to Hawkes's work:

"The entrance that was low and rounded and deep . . . the mouth of the fortress." The hell of the self is described as something not concrete ("You can't even smell it, boy") that recurs like a dream—"It's just a reflection—a reflection of some fiery nightmare." The journey downwards into the "penitential fortress" (*BO*, p. 191) is an act of regression. The deeper the couples go into the pervasive darkness, a darkness which suggests the unconscious ("the darkness was like the water in a cold well"), the younger they all seem to become: "We're like a bunch of kids" (*BO*, p. 194).

At the bottom of the fortress that is metaphor for Hugh's psyche, Hugh's puritanical core ("the dead breath of denial") is discovered, once again objectified in symbolic/metaphoric terms. The chastity belt, symbol of Hugh's repressive state of mind, is as much a product of dream, the subconscious, and the artistic imagination as it is of consciousness or reality: "It's there all right. I dreamed about it" (*BO*, p. 196). Perhaps the most interesting connection the chastity belt makes is between sexuality and the imagination of the failed artist; the belt, described as an "artful relic of fear and jealousy", makes the ultimate connection between Hugh the Man and Hugh the Artist through his repressive imagination.

Though Hawkes in interviews has championed Cyril as a "love singer", he seems to forget Cyril's description of the chastity belt as "smoldering, so to speak, with eroticism". Hawkes has said: "In *The Lime Twig* what Cyril would call 'sexual extension' (as opposed to 'wife swapping') is punished by death and total cataclysmic collapse, which is the mighty backlash of my own puritan upbringing . . . When I began *The Blood Oranges* I was quite aware of trying to write a fiction that . . . would give me an alternative to *The Lime Twig*" (Bellamy, p. 103). But Cyril's suggestion that "Hugh's despairing use of that iron belt must have occasioned a moment more genuinely erotic than any he had known" (*BO*, p. 257) is cause for alarm. Given the carrot eating scene in *Travesty* and Allert's voyeurism in *Death, Sleep and the Traveler*, the puritanism that Hawkes hoped to leave behind in *The Lime Twig* would seem to have survived in his continued depictions of repressed sexuality.

Signficantly, it is just at this juncture of eroticism and repression—the discovery of the chastity belt—that the bond between Cyril and Hugh is made clear: "Yes, I was Hugh's accomplice. In all my strength and weight I was not so very different from Hugh after all" (*BO*, p. 256). The element of repression Cyril shares with Hugh is reflected in his attitude toward women. Although Cyril views Fiona's extramarital pleasure with a grace uncharacteristic of the sexist, the position is inconsistent; there is something condescending if not repressive in Cyril's attitude toward women. Cyril speaks of "my omniscience and Fiona's style" (*BO*, p. 92), and he equates Fiona's imagination with what she can do in the kitchen: "How like Fiona on this morning of mornings to select from the garden of her imagination only those items which, according to superstition, were aphrodisiac. Just like Fiona to fuse in one stroke her feminine wisdom and my sensible view of sex" (*BO*, p. 261). Is Cyril's view of sex "sensible"? He views Fiona's clitoris as "the center of her life" (*BO*, p. 61), and when he describes Fiona as "the only woman I have ever known who, as sex aestheticism, was nearly my equivalent" (*BO*, p. 77), sexuality seems reduced to yet another function of male ego. Although Fiona is described as having "absolute self possession," Cyril, rather than trying to change Catherine, plays the authoritarian role, saying: "What Catherine doesn't know I tell her" (*BO*, p. 168). Paradox gives way to incon-

54

sistency. Although Cyril claims, "I am a match, I hope, for the hatred of conventional enemies whereever they are" (*BO*, p. 240), he says to Hugh: "There's nothing wrong with your marriage such as it is" (*BO*, p. 244). In spite of Cyril's claim: "Need I insist that the only enemy of the mature marriage is monogamy? That anything less than sexual multiplicity . . . is naive?" (*BO*, p. 209), he finally sides with Hugh: "To me fidelity is the most masculine trait of all" (*BO*, p. 4).

Whether one approves of Cyril or not, certainly he does not emerge as the Simon Bolivar of sexuality that he is made out to be. Though Hawkes was conscious of the connection between Cyril and Hugh—"polar opposites, versions of a single figure, they are both artists" (Bellamy, p. 101)—Cyril's view of women and the nature of his sexuality reflect upon the author, who continues to admire him: "[Cyril] may be unreliable or not, for me he is thoroughly accurate . . . exactly the kind of person I would be if . . . but I am not" (Kuehl, p. 176).

The image of the orange first appears as a bobbing symbol of consciousness in the canal by the side of the bus from which Hugh and his family emerge. The motion of the orange is a particularly apt image, for it suggests the motion of the narration, which floats along the narrator's consciousness in a present tense that so repeatedly dips into the past and leaps forward that the reader is left by this melange of time past, present, and future with the timeless sensation of a dream. The movement of the orange, like that of the ship in *Death, Sleep and the Traveler*, signals the spatial disorientation for the reader that links Hawkes with the vertical narratives of Joyce and Faulkner; his narration does not follow the horizontal plane of most of nineteenth-century fiction. At the end of the section about church, bus, and orange, one is prepared for the future—"I knew that we were due for some kind of new adventure, Fiona and I. What else could there be?"—but the next section plunges reader and narrator back into the past.

The use of dream in Hawkes's fiction is problematical. While dream and the unconscious are given freer rein in the early novels like *The Cannibal*, the essential difference between *The Blood Oranges* and the early books is the redefinition of reality as ongoing dream—"I recognized that I had already lived what Hugh might be dreaming" (*BO*, p. 85). For the reader as well as the author this has become part of a conscious process, the use of paradox in language and the breakdown of linear time no longer implicit but explicit in catch-phrases like "the nonsequential midafternoons in Illyria." Hawkes continues to float his fiction upwards on this sense of ongoing dream that separates him from the mainstream of American fiction. Just as Cyril voices his opposition to the conventional practice of marriage and other forms of behaviour that subdue the imagination, Hawkes voices his opposition to the conventionality of fictional realism: "Kuehl: When you think of a term like realism . . . Hawkes: It means pedestrian thinking. Kuehl: And pedestrian techniques? Hawkes: Yes" (Kuehl, p. 182). If *The Blood Oranges* is visionary fiction, it remains so in its understanding of the interdependence of imagination and sexuality, and in the weaving of time to convey a true sense of the ongoing dream of reality. The problem in *The Blood Oranges*, however, is that the idea of the weave breaks down. Given the pattern of images, Cyril's tapestry seems not so much like "weaving" as painting by numbers. Each character is given a color—Cyril gold and orange, Fiona yellow, Hugh black and white, Catherine white—which is meant to correspond to some aspect of their personality. Furthermore, Hugh, who as a photographer and puritan can only see life in clearly defined black and white, wears dark, heavy clothing that differentiates him from the light blues and whites of the other characters. The formula is as static as the symbol of the chastity belt. Movement, metaphoric mutation as suggested by Hester's "A" in *The Scarlet Letter*, is essential to a true romance weave.

Cyril's tapestry, while an apt description of the weave of images which characterizes *The Scarlet Letter* or Hawkes's early fiction, defeats the romance pattern to which it would speak. By raising to the surface and fixing to immobile meanings images that would have taken their metaphoric power from an unobtrusive association with other images and figures, Hawkes raises the local to the level of the universal, an end he has tried to accomplish in the trilogy without properly allowing for the vague intermediate step between word and metaphor.

DEATH, SLEEP AND THE TRAVELER

It is in the sense of just such a shift in process that *Death, Sleep and The Traveler*, the second novel in Hawkes's fictional triad dealing with love and the imagination, represents the dream turned inside out, the dream made conscious, the vision analyzed. If Cyril's experience in *The Blood Oranges* represents the living-out of Skipper's second, idyllic island, and the triumph of the imagination signalled through the liberation of a mind now capable of creating a world in which sexuality represents joy rather than repression, *Death*, anticipating the suicide/murder of the artist/man in *Travesty*, represents a thorough examination of a consciousness whose obsession with the "self" clearly establishes Dream as the hypotenuse stretching across the angle of intersection between Love and the Imagination.

The reflexive creative act of *Death, Sleep and The Traveler* involves a reexamination of a great deal of Hawkes's fictional territory, and a reutilisation of a number of earlier images, themes, and narrative preoccupations. Frederick Busch says of *Death*, "It is as if he (Hawkes) were trying to pull together the strands of psychic line which he has spun over twenty-five years of writing" (Insights-I, p. 59).

Though the narratives of the first two novels of the triad differ—Cyril, the life singer, is in opposition to Allert, who experiences (in Hawkes's words) "in his own psyche his own death" (*TREMA*, p. 264)—there are thematic and metaphoric connections, the most obvious of which is Allert's connection to Hugh, the photographer in *The Blood Oranges*. Both Hugh and Allert are victims of Image worship, and both are pornographers, Allert's young nymphet, Ariane, being the realization in fantasy form of Hugh's peasant nudes. The essential difference between them is that Allert is trying to "realize" his fantasies—unlike Hugh, he does not repress his desire; rather, he becomes intent on possessing Ariane as if sexuality were a means of making her real. Furthermore, with Allert the emphasis shifts from the Image to the man behind the image, the man behind the camera's eye. The photograph of "two small naked figures" is not only the key to Allert's voyeuristic sexuality and past, but also the point at which photography and voyeurism meet in Image, the product of the observer and the observed, and the key to Allert's narration. First mentioned in connection with Allert's first recollection of sexuality, the picture Allert sees reflected in the barber's mirror, of a boy on a bicycle watching a young, nude girl posing for a picture, depicts the observer (the boy on the bicycle) observed (by young Allert). The effect on the ultimate observer is, in Allert's words, that "the mirror and the photograph are drawing closer" (*DST*, p. 50), image and reality blurring inextricably in the mind of the observer, as are, for the adult Allert, Sexuality and Imagination.

The narrative develops Allert's sexuality and imagination on three levels which disrupt fixed notions of Time and Space by the weaving of the three. The narrative blends psychic Past (Allert's remembrances and dreams, told in the immediacy of the present tense), with a seemingly surface Reality (though told in the past tense, the level at which Ursula's analysis of Allert's dreams gives both Allert and the reader the illusion of an actuality), and thirdly and most dramatically, the Time-Space continuum of Romance (the level of Allert's voyage with Ariane, the result of his sexual desires and frustrations and his imagination, "real" primarily in the sense that the voyage is suggested by Ursula). The narrative perspective is no longer as simple as that suggested by the lighthouse on Skipper's shoulders. The three levels of time-space are projected in front of the reader in two triangles: the "fantasy" triangle of Allert-Ariane-Olaf is the negative of the developed marital picture we have of Allert-Ursula and Peter. The failure of Olaf's rivalry foreshadows Peter's death; both women disappear—Ariane is murdered, wife Ursula leaves; Allert is left with the present tense of his dreams. Certainly the three levels of reality encountered in the narration—the levels reflecting the fictional process through which idea becomes negative (image) and is developed (into metaphor)—are the key to both the fragmented narration and the intricacies of Allert's mind.

If Allert emerges as an artist, it is because his survival ultimately depends on his ability to assimilate the seemingly disparate parts of his "self," a self which, objectified by narrative distance, is a model for the spatial/temporal disorientation that the reader also suffers. Allert's "inability to believe in the reality of the human self" (*DST*, p. 90) is the position of the imaginative artist caught between the three levels of consciousness, subconscious, and unconscious. Indeed, Ursula sees Allert not as an artist but as the primal dreamer, the child in the womb: "You have the face of a fetus. Perhaps that is why you dream rather than live your life" (*DST*, p. 75). As narrator Allert finally controls the fiction of his self. He makes, as Robert Steiner suggests, "an ultimate distinction between fantasy, dream and actuality", and, having murdered Peter, the analyst who Allert watches having sex with his wife, Allert proclaims "I am not guilty." Whether he is reprehensible or personally grotesque, the success of Allert as narrator is intended to be this denial of morality.

In *Death, Sleep and The Traveler* survival has become a question which inextricably links artist, narrator, and reader: survival has become a question of distancing and imposition of forms. Allert's problem is distinguishing between Dream and Reality as reflected in the three-tiered narration ultimately represents the same voyage of self discovery that Skipper experienced, though here the analysis becomes conscious, whereas in *Second Skin* understanding remained primarily intuitive, realization at the subconscious level reflected in a change of the course of Skipper's actions. Allert does not change, he just survives. Nonetheless, Allert's problem becomes the reader's problem, largely because the shifting planes of narrative reality engage the reader in Allert's creative problem of perception: what at first appears to be the most concrete reality, Ursula's level, is at times just as imaginary as the voyage and the dreams.

The Island and the Ship (the metaphoric vehicle in *Second Skin*) appear to offer the potential for growth that is the key to Romance imagery and metaphor.

But whereas the Island as idea in *Second Skin* undergoes a profound change with metaphoric consequences for Skipper, who experiences both the cold Atlantic and Catalina Kate's island in his search for a peaceful paradise within himself, the single island encountered in *Death*, obviously intended to be an imaginary/psychological metaphor, remains instead a static fixity.

What, however, does this fantasy island represent? The immediate answer, suggested by Allert's drawing back of "the green curtain across my porthole" (*DST*, p. 52), is that the island represents sexual freedom; indeed, it is said to be inhabited only by nudists. Significant in terms of Allert's repressed sexuality, the middle-aged man does not even realize the island is there; he must have it pointed out to him by his nymphet, Ariane. Allert's response to the island—" 'It is only an island after all,' I said evenly, 'it is not Atlantis' " (*DST*, p. 52)—reveals Allert's nature as man and artist. At this point Allert's imagination is sterile: he sees only an island like the one Skipper encountered with Cassandra, a "dry, treeless and apparently heartshaped knoll" (*DST*, p. 54); he fails to recognize the potential of the Imagination in creating the mind's own paradise; he fails to understand why the goats can survive on the island without food—"It's because they're unreal, Allert. That's why" (*DST*, p. 55)—and he fails to recognize Ariane's imaginative, artistic potential.

Skipper's voyage has more than a symbolic function, for he is captain of the Starfish, a fact which makes the self's voyage (mutiny, attack, and lifeboats) work on more than one level. In *Death* Hawkes no longer lets the reader make the essential connections to create the metaphor for himself; rather, Hawkes presents the reader with the metaphor as a *fait accompli*. By making the ship an obvious metaphor—"feeling the stasis of the ship in my own large body" (*DST*, p. 7), "the ship's pool which was a parody of the sea it travelled on" (*DST*, p. 16)—the metaphor never really gets out of the port of the writer's understanding.

Nonetheless, the ship remains an important fixity in *Death*. The sea is parodied by the ship's pool, and Allert's swim—"I, with lungs distended and eyes open, began to descend . . . to the bottom . . . I knew I was quite alone in the pool . . . suddenly I had in fact achieved the bottom . . . " (*DST*, pp. 32-3) represents man going down into the waters of the self. Hawkes suggests this is the central action of the novel: "*Death, Sleep and the Traveler* is in fact a fiction about a man descending inside himself in order to experience in his own psyche his own death, in the process of which he is of course experiencing the riches of the imagination" (*TREMA*, p. 264). This voyage of the self is necessary for the survival of the individual, particularly the creative individual, for, as Allert says, "I myself am my only access to what I want to know" (*DST*, p. 138). It is Peter, the analyst, who serves as Hawkes's mouthpiece when he tells Allert that "sinking into the depths of darkness, drowning in the sea of the self" is necessary to the individual's rebirth, for, "the greater the agony with which he approached oblivion, then the greater and more profound and more joyous his recovery, his rebirth" (*DST*, p. 143).

Although Hawkes recognizes that Allert's psyche is somehow diseased, that Allert's rash is a metaphor for what is inside him, like the disease Cap Leech found in the palm of the Sheriff's hand ("I have never known such a rash and could not have imagined any skin condition capable of so much change and such determined growth" [*BL*, p. 145]); and although the writer self consciously makes excuses for his narrator's behavior through Ursula's criticism of his dreams and language and romantic vision with statements like, " 'Allert,' she said, 'I wish you'd stop poeticizing my crotch'," the fundamental problems of *Death* revolve around the question of distance between Hawkes and this narrator whom he likes.

Allert's absorption with himself is surely why Ursula, herself a strong but graceless woman (" 'But Peter's in his prime, Allert. That's what I mean' " [*DST*, p. 87]), leaves him; and from the beginning, Allert's voyage of the self is also an ego-trip: "the young woman had herself selected me from all the passengers" (*DST*, p. 8). Ursula says to Allert early on, "the trouble with you is that you are a psychic invalid. You have no feeling" (*DST*, pp 8-9). Allert admits: "I am a deliberate fetishist" (*DST*, p. 173). But while his narrative role as observer accounts somewhat for his voyeurism, Allert's main problem is his lack of passion for anyone but himself. The fetishistic scene in which Ariane, in the nude, plays a flute described as a "silver snake" moves Allert first to masturbation rather than love-making; and Allert's interest in the origins of his first erection, coupled with his enjoyment in watching Peter make love to Ursula, suggest that his phallic obsession ("In my dream I am somehow endowed with the rare North Penis" [*DST*, p. 16]) has onanistic overtones. Indeed, at the zoo Allert is particularly taken by "the slow jerky calisthenics of autofellatio" (*DST*, p. 124) being performed by two bats, and says that "in my slowness I contained the desperation of the two bats." Perhaps Ursula's excuse to Peter is accurate: " 'Allert,' she replied at once, 'is not interested in homosexuals. Unless they are women' " (*DST*, p. 152). Allert is not a homosexual, but he is mired in the ambiguities of sexual paradox, stuck where narrator and voyeur are one: "the ordinary man becomes an artist only in sex. In which case pornography is the true field of the ordinary man's imagination" (*DST*, p. 153).

Allert's relationship to Ariane is based largely on the formula Cyril warned Hugh against: woman as Image. Ariane exists largely in Allert's imagination: "I did not need to open my eyes to know she was there, since I could see her with my eyes quite shut" (*DST*, p. 34); and what Allert appreciates most about her is her youth. In part the attraction of youth is Innocence, a notion Hawkes clings to in spite of the fact that it is the aspect of purity within Innocence that is behind Hugh's puritanism; also, Allert is attracted to young Ariane because unlike the wise Ursula, the young nymphet strokes his ego, gives him the illusion of strength: "I am not going into the pool today. It's too rough. I am not as strong as you are" (*DST*, p. 34). It is apparently sufficient for Allert that Ariane exist as a function of his fantasy; she need not be any more real than that, for Allert sees her as "an anonymous female figure" (*DST*, p. 45).

The island Allert and Ariane visit is, to use Allert's phrase, part of "the unmoving fictional horizon" (*DST*, p. 9). But the difference between Hawkes's sense of imaginary in this instance and the reality that in Borges's stories often seems part of Someone's Fiction (for example, the traitorous Irish leader who agrees to play out his role as martyr, to be murdered like Julius Caesar for the citizens who are all actors, all unwittingly part of the play) is important: Hawkes fails here to take Borges's additional step back from the idea.

Allert's phrase "the unmoving fictional horizon" is the key to the shift in Hawkes's work that the triad represents. By means of an increasingly self-conscious first person narrator, Hawkes has raised his images and metaphors to the surface, a shift which to the reader familiar with Hawkes's earlier works amounts to the author's examination of images and patterns more alive, less clearly the subject of analysis, than in his early Romance Novels.

There is a certain irony in the fact that Hawkes calls *The Blood Oranges, Death, Sleep and the Traveler*, and *Travesty* his "triad" of fictions rather than a "trilogy," emphasizing the way in which his ideas about the self, the artist, and the romantic vision are woven and echoed as the imagery of a poem rather than dramatized (the more novelistic approach) with a cast of characters. That Hawkes consciously planned the triad can readily be proved by an examination of theme, and through various cross references between the novels. In *Death*, we have seen connections which refer back to Tremlow and Skipper of *Second Skin*. There are cursory connections—the way in which Allert and Peter refer to each other in direct address as "my friend" and the way in which Papa refers to his silent passenger, Henri, as "cher ami"—and there are more fundamental connections. Allert not only foreshadows the landscape of *Travesty*, but also the psychic position from which the narrator of *Travesty* begins his journey when he says: "I know where I am going, I am in possession of myself, and yet I know too that I have no history, no recollection of the past, so that my life, which is specific, depends only on the field, the ditch, the night and what I am about to experience within the chateau: I know the way. There is nothing else" (*DST*, p. 73). There is also a further connection between Hawkes's last two novels; what we have recognized in the early novels as romance novel techniques have largely been abandoned for a type of dramatic monologue more closely aligned to the novel proper; Hawkes continues to discard many novelistic techniques, refusing to build standard dramatic narrative tension. In both *Death* ("I received my all-too-accurate premonition that Peter's life was going to end, when that moment came, in the sauna" [*DST*, p. 24]) and in *Travesty* ("Not many young women have the opportunity of passing their last minutes in the company of love and loving Papa both" [*T*, p. 12]), the reader is told almost immediately of potentially dramatic events that many novels build toward, thus placing the emphasis not on drama but on idea.

Far more in *Travesty* than in *Death*, the narrative exists at the level of the conscious; and though Papa makes reference to "all those earliest sensations of fear and security" (*T*, p. 28), these are not dramatized as products of the subconscious, but rather addressed directly as part of the surface landscape. There remain, nonetheless, elements that tie *Travesty* to the early work and the other parts of the trilogy. Papa's wife and Henri's lover, Honorine, not only shares this dual role (as does Ursula in *Death*), but Papa's final description of Honorine, "the lady of the dark chateau" (*T*, p. 122), as "being her typically unsentimental self" recalls not only Ursula but the character who prefigured her in *Second Skin*, Miranda. This "unsentimental" side of Honorine seems to result from the death of their son, Pascal, a death whose memory suggests an end to a certain type of reasoning, but also the life and sexual freedom suggested by Cyril's grape arbour in *The Blood Oranges*: "until his rosy and sturdy little buttocks were firmly, squarely in place atop Honorine's cluster of purple grapes. There he would sit . . . How did Honorine survive his death. How did I?" (*T*, p. 89). Most important to understanding the narrative departure *Travesty* represents within Hawkes's work is the movie house, which sounds strangely like the theatre where Madame Snow's crippled son entertained himself in *The Cannibal*: "If the invisible camera existed, and if it recorded this adventure of ours from beginning to end, and if the reel of film were salvaged and then late one night its images projected onto a tattered white screen in some movie house smelling of disinfectant and damp clothing and containing almost no audience at all, it is then that your malignant admirers would stand in the cold aisles and dismiss me as a silly coward and condemn you as a worthless soul" (*T*, p. 80). The reference to camera and theatre is of primary interest, given Hawkes's concern with focus and distance, an interest that has grown out of the binoculars in *The Lime Twig* into the lighthouse on Skipper's shoulders in *Second Skin* into the kaleidoscopic vision and existence portrayed in *Death*. In *Travesty*, all lenses are brought to absolute zero: there is no longer the question or the possibility of depth perception; Papa's face, like those of the passengers of his mind, is pressed flat against the windshield of his vehicle.

Papa, the otherwise unnamed narrator of *Travesty*, is unlike any of the narrators or characters previously encountered in Hawkes; there is no sense here of seeking personal or artistic salvation through the ongoing process of survival. In *Travesty* the self is past questing, the narrator not primarily the artist figure, but Man on the brink of extinction. The inference is that the creative act no longer primarily involves creation but its polar mate, destruction, the ultimate existential moment for Artist and Man being the collision between vehicle and stone wall, in which the impact between Life and Death is felt most intensely and then not at all.

The inevitable collision accounts in part for the remarkable fact that in *Travesty* narrator and narrative are absolutely one. Papa *is* the narrative, a position one can find as well in Barth's "Story for Tape," or Barthelme's story "Sequence." Each curve in the road, each acceleration or shift in the prose is a function of Papa's imagination and memory: "I am aware of a particular distance; these yellow headlights are the lights of my eyes; my mind is bound inside my memory of this curving road like a fist in glass" (*T*, p. 15).

Like all of Hawkes's novels, *Travesty* is built on paradox the most central of which is apparently resolvable only in the crash which represents an ultimate synthesis (the death of the Man an end as well to Artist and narration); this is the paradox that sets Imagination against Memory. Papa is creating but he is also destroying. The destructive element in the narrative creative act is a function of memory. After each scene or anecdote recalled in the past tense, the narrative accelerates forward toward death in the present tense: "Time passed like ivory beads on a black thread. My own blood climbed inside the glass. Again I had my brief affair with the old X-ray machine . . . " (p. 94) "Yes, she is vomiting . . . " (p. 95) "A trifle faster? Yes, you are right that we are now travelling a breath or two faster than we were . . . " (p. 96) (*T* pp. 94-96).

In *Travesty*, the symmetry born of paradox and conflict is no longer a possibility or a goal. The narrator of *Travesty* has abandoned the psychic and structural tightrope of Paradox for a road with a sure ending. Nonetheless, there is still evidence—the points at which Cyril and Allert exist in the narrator of *Travesty*—that Papa sees his world, particularly his past, in terms of paradox: "Suddenly you and I are more different than ever, yet closer even than we were three to a bed" (*T*, p. 17); "that olive tree is beautiful only because it is so deformed" (*T*, p. 29). Greiner points out that, "Papa expresses his fascination with the harmony of paradox in various ways. He knows, o example, little about cars, yet drives them well. He cannot tolerate the ticking of Honorine's clock, yet hears it loudest when he jams the mechanism. He enjoys the meeting of the crow, the bird of death, and the canary, the bird of song A connoisseur

61

of fine automobiles, he is nevertheless attracted to crash sites . . . Similarly, he is equally entranced by photographs of lovely nudes and by pictures of 'the most brutal and uncanny destructions of human flesh' '' (*Insights*, p. 151). But there is no "harmony of paradox" in the crash Papa is heading for. Death resolves paradox not in harmony, but in death. Papa is less interested in trying to survive through discovering the harmony of paradox than in experiencing (and revealing for the reader) the limits of existence, the existential point of intersection of Man and Artist.

Papa's relationship to Henri, the poet/passenger, is the cornerstone of the novel. Henri's passivity and the way in which he is addressed as "you" suggests that he represents the reader, who is also forced to travel with Papa. Henri's silence suggests that he is a projection of Papa's imagination. Though Papa claims, "I am no poet" (*T*, p. 14), he seems to have the mind and preoccupations of an artist—Papa has a "nearly phobic yearning for the truest paradox, a thirst to lie at the center of this paradigm," and a disdain for those incapable of seeing, as he can, the local in terms of metaphor: "The triteness of a nation incapable of understanding highway, motor vehicle, pedestrian" (*T*, p. 19). Papa further suggests a bond with Henri when he says "In my youth I also had my taste or two of that 'cruel detachment' which was to make you famous" (*T*, pp. 47-8)—a line which describes Hawkes's own proclaimed "detachment." The bond between Man and Artist becomes inextricable by the end of the book when the image of poet as criminal ("the poet is always a betrayer, a murderer, and that the writing of poetry is like a descent into death" [*T*, p. 80]) is reprised: "Perhaps the privileged man is an even greater criminal than the poet" (*T*, p. 127). Indeed Papa, though perhaps "not guilty" like Allert, has already abducted Henri and Chantal, and is about to commit murder (as well as suicide) when this "criminal" quotes two lines from Henri's poetry; he comments, "I am extremely fond of these two lines. I might even have written them myself" (*T*, p. 127).

Papa's imaginative relationship to Henri is the model for his relationship to the other figures; all the reader knows of Chantal, Honorine, and Monique is what the narrator tells us. The reader is faced with the problem, ripe with unused metaphoric possibilities of an unreliable narrator who is also omniscient—and in this sense Papa is an artist, his existence a work of art, for he creates, as in a sense we all do, the population of his existence. The women in Papa's world are born at the junction of imagination and sexuality, and Papa, whose name is a reflection of his authoritarianism (the father insists upon absolute control, he gives orders to his captive passengers), seems attracted to them individually to the degree that they stimulte his imagination (his wife, the least; his daughter, the most).

Papa's sexuality is a function of his imagination (as all sexuality is), and this sexuality, in keeping with the imagination that creates the vehicle of suicide/murder, is essentially frustrated and destructive. Of central importance to understanding Papa's repressed sexual imagination is the fact that Papa, like Hugh and Allert before him in the triad, still would see woman as an Image of Innocence. Honorine, who as wife is largely disregarded by comparison to the attention Papa pays mistress and daughter, poses in the nude for Papa's camera: though not captivating as woman/wife or as an image, Honorine can stimulte Papa's imagination. Monique, the mistress, is even more a product of the pornographer's imagination, for Papa describes her as the amalgamation of "all the uninhibited nudes I courted in pornographic magazines of my own late and isolated boyhood" (*T*, p. 67). As pornographic fantasy, Monique is linked to Papa's own daughter, Chantal, who is called the "porno brat." a connection further supported by the spanking Papa adminsters to Monique, a public humiliation which speaks to Papa's own sexual frustration. It is Papa's treatment of Monique as a child that underscores the fantasy running through the triad of woman as Innocence. All of the "heroines" in the triad (Catherine, Fiona, and especially Ariane and Monique) have something of childish innocence about them, as if "youth" means "purity"; whereas the adult women (Ursula and Honorine) are mature in years and somehow deathly, like Miranda in *Second Skin*. But this vision of the image of Innocence, as evidenced by Hugh's sexually frustrating dependence on the Image, is doubly perverse, because though a father's attraction for his daughter is natural, this desire is never admitted but is suppressed as a function of the imagination seen in Allert's equation of imagination and pornography: "pornography is the true field of the ordinary man's imagination" (*DST*, p. 153).

There are elements of incest in the pornographer's fascination with his daughter. Papa enjoys being able to lick chocolate off Chantal's fingers with "perfect impunity" (a suggestion that Papa is doing something that he should not); and later, even though his wife is with him, Papa has difficulty suppressing his envy of the young restaurant owner ("The black pointed tip of his shoe was visible between her knees, he crouched behind her like a ventriloquist manipulating an erotic doll" [*T*, p. 118]) presiding over the implicitly sexual carrot eating contest. Papa obviously enjoys the fact that the young girls are bound: "all three girls knelt as one with their faces raised, their knees apart, and their hands behind their upright backs. The tips of the immense carrots hung barely within reach of the three sets of pretty lips . . . they began to grope for the tips of the carrots with their open mouths, with their bright red girlish lips now puckered into an oval shape, or at last and skilfully enough to begin to fish desperately for the fat carrots with their glistening tongues" (*T*, p. 116-18). Some may find such a description imaginative or erotic, but it is essentially repressed. Furthermore, the purpose of imagination—as Hawthorne's work is testament—is not simply to fantasize but to aid the individual in seeing things as they really are. Papa outlines his fantasy—"these three young, innocent girls were already more provocative, more indiscreetly revealed, than most professional semi-nude girls in a chorus line" (*T*, p. 115)—but he never succeeds in relating his suppressed desires to his situation. Papa's imagination fails him. He would prefer to view it all as part of a summer of a "certain harmless decadence," but his refusal to admit why he is interested in Chantal's mouth around the carrot gives his account of the gesture its air of repressed morality. Thus, Papa's notion of Innocence is perverse primarily because he refuses to acknowledge the natural, if incestuous, attraction of father for daughter, the artist/man instead suppressing desire in Image, an image called Innocence. This seems to minimize the guilt.

Travesty presents the reader with several unresolvable paradoxes. First, if there is to be a crash with "no survivors," how is the fiction created, who transcribes the narration? This first problem is linked with a verbal impossibility: the narrator is *planning an accident*. In terms of its effect on the prose, perhaps the most telling paradox is that, although for the first time one of Hawkes's narrators seems in charge both of the narrative and his own fate, Papa's position of ultimate control remains, like Zizendorf's, essentially authoritarian: lines like "Another cigarette. I approve" (*T*, p. 37) or "You must obey your

Papa" (*T*, p. 11) grow into sweeping statements like "No man is guilty of any-thing, whatever he does" (*T*, p. 36).

Ironically, the narrator's failure to arrive at another end than the wall repre-sents ultimately a failure of the imagination. But how exactly does Hawkes intend this irony? Since none of the other passengers or characters speak even in Papa's recollection of them, there is the possibility that these figures (and even the drive itself) do not exist except as they move in the mind of a man whose psychic past, it must be remembered, is driving him to self-destruction. If *Travesty* is purely imaginary in this sense, then this "triad of fictions about sexuality and the romantic imagination in an absurdist world" runs the risk of turning Hawkes's fiction into an intellectual exercise.

BIOGRAPHY & BIBLIOGRAPHY

John Clendennin Burne Hawkes, Jr., was born August 17, 1925, in Stamford, Conn., the son of John & Helen Hawkes. After receiving his A.B. from Harvard University in 1949, Hawkes became an assistant to the Production Manager at Harvard University Press; he has since taught at Harvard, Brown Univer-sity, and MIT. He is married, with four children. Among his many honors is a Master's Degree from Brown University. A list of his published books follows:

1. *Fiasco Hall*. Privately printed, Cambridge, Mass., 1943, 14p, Paper, Verse
2. *The Cannibal*. New Directions, New York, 1949, 223p, Cloth, Novel
3. *The Beetle Leg*. New Directions, New York, 1951, 159p, Cloth, Novel
4. *The Goose on the Grave; The Owl; 2 Short Novels*. New Directions, New York, 1954, 207p, Cloth, Coll.
5. *The Lime Twig*. New Directions, New York, 1961, 175p, Cloth, Novel
6. *Second Skin*. New Directions, New York, 1964, 210p, Cloth, Novel
7. *The Innocent Party; Four Plays*. New Directions, New York, 1967, 239p, Cloth, Drama Coll.
8. *Lunar Landscapes; Stories & Short Novels, 1949-1963*. New Directions, New York, 1969, 275p, Cloth, Coll.
9. *The Blood Oranges*. New Directions, New York, 1971, 271p, Cloth, Novel
10. *Death, Sleep & the Traveler*. New Directions, New York, 1974, 179p, Cloth, Novel
11. *Travesty*. New Directions, New York, 1976, 128p, Cloth, Novel